The Journey Isn't Over

The Journey Isn't Over

The Pilgrim Psalms for Life's Challenges and Joys

Walter C. Kaiser, Jr.

BAKER BOOK HOUSE
Grand Rapids, Michigan 49516

Library of Congress Cataloging-in-Publication Data

Kaiser, Walter C.
  The journey isn't over: the pilgrim Psalms for life's challenges and
joys/Walter C. Kaiser, Jr.
    p. cm.
    ISBN 0-8010-5258-0
    1. Bible. O.T. Psalms CXX-CXXXIV—Meditations. I. Title. II. Title:
Journey isn't over.
BS1430.4.K35 1993
223'.206—dc20
                                                        92-31660

Other Books by the Author

Classical Evangelical Essays in Old Testament Interpretation (editor) (o.p.)
The Old Testament in Contemporary Preaching (o.p.)
Toward an Old Testament Theology
Ecclesiastes: Total Life
*Toward an Exegetical Theology: Biblical Exegesis for Preaching and
    Teaching*
A Biblical Approach to Personal Suffering: Studies in Lamentations
Toward Old Testament Ethics
Malachi: God's Unchanging Love (o.p.)
The Uses of the Old Testament in the New (o.p.)
Quest for Renewal: Personal Revival in the Old Testament (o.p.)
Quality Living: Bible Studies in Ecclesiastes (o.p.)
A Tribute to Gleason Archer: Essays in Old Testament Studies (co-editor)
    (o.p.)
Have You Seen the Power of God Lately? Studies in the Life of Elijah (o.p.)
Toward Rediscovering the Old Testament
Hard Sayings of the Old Testament
"Exodus" in *The Expositor's Bible Commentary*
Back Twoard the Future: Hints for Interpreting Biblical Prophecy
More Hard Sayings of the Old Testament
The Communicator's Commentary: Micah to Malachi
"Leviticus" in *The New Interpreter's Bible* (forthcoming)

A special word of appreciation must be given to a stalwart group of friends that met every Thursday night through the winter and spring of 1990 to journey through these Psalms of Ascent. For their joy in the study of God's Word, their friendly criticisms of the material contained herein, and their encouragement of each other toward growth in our Lord, this volume is dedicated with strong affections in Christ and deep appreciation for these fellow pilgrims from The Village of Lincolnshire, Illinois:

Chris Cool
Marshall Cool
Carl England
Jeanne England
Cole Hanner
Pam Hanner
Marge Kaiser
June Seaberg
Jean Soderberg
Rich Soderberg
Connie Warwick
Ron Warwick
Betty Weimar

Contents

Preface

Daydreaming while at the wheel of a vehicle may bring a sudden rebuke from another motorist: "Stay in your own lane!" How important that same reminder is for those of who have begun to journey with the Lord of heaven.

The apostle Paul gave a similar reminder when he defended his own ministry: "We, however, will not boast beyond proper limits, but will confine our boasting to the lane God has assigned [or marked out] to us" (2 Cor. 10:13 NIV, with author's change). The Greek word Paul used here is *kanonos,* or our word canon, a lane or reed that is used as a standard for what is normative and what is not.

The fifteen psalms included in this study are for those people who will spend life going with the Lord in the distinctive lane that he has marked out for each of us. All too often people want to jump over into someone else's lane and take up that person's journey and identity. But the person who is truly apprenticed to the Lord Jesus Christ will spend his or her days growing and following the master. And that life will be filled with song.

These fifteen psalms will amaze you. They are so intensely practical, so wide-ranging in their scope of topics, and so eminently down to earth in what they have to teach us about our walk with God, whether that walk takes us to the marketplace, the home, or the nation.

Included in this study are questions for your thought and reflection. You might enjoy using these issues as probes for your own home Bible-study group, as an elective course in the educational program of your local church, or as a basis for a dorm Bible-study and prayer group.

After each chapter I have included the poetic interpretation for each of these psalms that Isaac Watts set to music. (I became aware of this wonderful heritage from the volume *The Poetic Interpretation of Psalms by Isaac Watts*, by N. A. Woychuck.) I am convinced that until we learn to repeat back to God the anthems of his Word in great doxology, we shall know only in an analytical and a fragmentary way the theology contained in his Word, and therefore I suggest that you or your group sing these psalms after you have studied them.

Isaac Watts worked for some nineteen years "to accommodate the Book of Psalms to Christian worship." Utilizing the language of the New Testament, he set the psalms in easy metrical verse so that they could be sung in private and public worship. He toiled while bearing up under a prolonged illness, and his completed work was published in 1719 under the long title, *The Psalms of David Imitated in the Language of the New Testament and Applied to the Christian State and Worship*. His work covered 138 entire psalms, most of them rendered in two or three different meters. Only 12 psalms were omitted and a few included only parts of a psalm. More than four thousand copies of Watts's work were sold within one year of its publication; by his death in 1748 there had been seven editions of the *Psalms*.

I am grateful to Miracle Press, which published this volume in 1974, for permission to quote Watts's poetic interpretation of these psalms. The meters for the suggested tunes are as follows:

Common Meter (abbreviated C.M.)

Alas, and Did My Savior Bleed
All Hail the Power of Jesus' Name

Amazing Grace
Joy to the World
O for a Thousand Tongues to Sing
Am I a Soldier of the Cross
Majestic Sweetness Sits Enthroned

Short Meter (abbreviated S.M.)

Blest Be the Tie That Binds
Crown Him with Many Crowns
Rejoice, Ye Pure in Heart
I Love Thy Kingdom, Lord
A Charge to Keep I Have
O Bless the Lord, My Soul
Come, We That Love the Lord

Long Meter (abbreviated L.M.)

Jesus Shall Reign
Praise God from Whom All Blessings Flow
Just as I Am
The Solid Rock
Jesus, Thou Joy of Loving Hearts
Sun of My Soul
Give to Our God Immortal Praise
When I Survey the Wondrous Cross

Beside those friends mentioned in the dedication, I would like to express my appreciation for those assisting me, especially Jan M. Ortiz and my editor at Baker, Linda Triemstra. And my best friend and encourager is my wife, Marge. She has helped in many of the tasks connected with the production of this volume. To you the reader, I commend this work with a prayer for the blessing of God on your life as you read it.

Introduction

The fifteen psalms from Psalm 120 to 134 are a small hymnal within the larger one, just as a number of other groupings such as the Hallelujah Psalms (146–150) or the Kingship Psalms (93–100) function within the whole Psalter.

But the fact that psalms 120–134 are a separate and consecutive collection should not detract from the recently rediscovered observation that each of these individual psalms and collections have a relationship to each other and are probably placed side by side for an overall purpose. In the case of these fifteen psalms, they are preceded by Psalm 119, the longest psalm of all, which describes the richness of the law of God that will go before the pilgrim wherever he or she shall go. Psalms 135–137, which come immediately after the collection, appear to supplement their theme.

Psalms 120–134 are unique in that each has the heading, though slightly varied in Psalm 121, which functions as the name for the group. The problem, however, is that there is little agreement on exactly what that title means. Most will agree that the title is a feminine noun related to the verb *to go up*. But what is it that is going up?

Some believe that the reference to "going up" is literary; therefore they relate it either to the steplike parallelism in the text, where so many lines appear to be echoed in the second line, or to the praising character of these psalms ("extolments"). Neither designation fits all fifteen psalms, nor are these psalms unique in either category.

One of the most frequently heard suggestions is the one that relates the fifteen psalms to the fifteen steps leading up from the Court of the Women to the Court of Israel in the temple. Each step, it is alleged, corresponds to one psalm in this collection. Beginning with the first day of the Feast of Tabernacles, the Levites would sing the song derived from these psalms as they mounted all fifteen steps. The Hebrew *Mishnah* (*Middoth* 2.5) preserved the tradition in this manner: "Fifteen steps led up from within it (i.e., the court of the women) to the court of the Israelites, corresponding to the fifteen Songs of Ascent in the Psalms, and upon them the Levites used to sing." No record exists to prove that the Levites sang these psalms as described here. Likewise, the Hebrew *Mishnah* (tractate *Sukkah* 5.4) gave a parallel account: "And countless Levites played on harps, lyres, cymbals and trumpets and instruments of music, on the fifteen steps leading down from the court of the Israelites to the court of the women, corresponding to the fifteen Songs of Ascents in the Psalms." It is difficult to know if these are two independent sources or if they are dependent on each other or a common source. Both, however, connect the fifteen steps in the temple with the fifteen Psalms of Ascent. Both use the phrase *corresponding to.*

A different solution was posited by L. J. Liebreich in 1955. He agreed that the phrase *going up* referred to the "steps" of the temple porch, but argued that each of the fifteen psalms was an elaboration of one of the key terms in the Aaronic benediction of Numbers 6:24–26:

> The Lord bless you
>   and keep you;
> the Lord make his face shine upon you
>   and be gracious to you;
> the Lord turn his face toward you
>   and give you peace.

Unfortunately for this creative suggestion, three of the psalms—124, 126, and 131—do not contain one of the key words from this benediction. Nevertheless, it is indeed striking how close is the relationship of that priestly blessing from the Pentateuch to most of these psalms.

Most recent commentators settle for the view that the verb *to go up* is used for pilgrimages (e.g., Ps. 24:3; Isa. 2:3). The "ascents" referred to here would be those made by the Israelites as they journeyed to Jerusalem to celebrate the three great festivals each year: Passover, at the beginning of the wheat harvest; Pentecost, at the end of the wheat harvest; and Rosh Hashanah, or New Year's, when the grapes were gathered. Presumably, these songs were sung along the way and marked the progress of the journey and the concerns of heart as the pilgrim remembered those at home and entered into the joy of the city of Zion. Most will point to Isaiah 30:29 to substantiate such a view:

> And you will sing
> > as on the night you celebrate a holy festival;
> your hearts will rejoice
> > as when people go up with flutes
> to the mountain of the LORD,
> > to the Rock of Israel.

It is clear that the verb *to go up* was often used of the processional ascent to the temple (2 Sam. 6:12, 15; 1 Kings 13:33; 2 Kings 23:2; Pss. 24; 42:4; 100; Isa. 26:2; 30:29). E. Lipinski associated the steps with the stairway at the Fountain Gate, which was on the processional route leading to the temple (Neh. 12:37). Thus he too saw these psalms as "songs of the stairway."

For all their brevity, it can certainly be said that these fifteen psalms are preoccupied with "Zion." Seven of the fifteen contain the term (125, 126, 128, 129, 132, 133, 134). Psalm 122 uses "Jerusalem" instead, while 121, 123, and 124 have formulations that are associated with Zion. Only 120, 127, 130, and 131 do not appear to be directly related to this tally.

Luther took a different tack. He translated the title as songs to be sung in an elevated or a high place, such as a choir; a place where access was gained only by means of steps. In confirmation of this translation he pointed to 2 Chronicles 20:19, which says the Levites praised God with a loud voice "on high." However, Luther failed to notice that the Hebrew form actually functioned as an adverb, not a noun. In other places, Luther suggested that these were "psalms of rising up" (i.e., psalms to be sung at the conclusion of the service as the congregation was departing). He also conjectured that they were "songs in a high key" (i.e., not of musical pitch, but hymns of joy and exaltation).

John Lightfoot and E. Thirtle advanced the suggestion that these psalms were connected with King Hezekiah and the steps were actually degrees on the sundial of King Ahaz that retreated ten steps (2 Kings 20:10). The arguments for this thesis are that King Hezekiah employed a company of men who transcribed and copied the sacred text (Prov. 25:1); Hezekiah was a poet, as his composition in Isaiah 38:10–20 demonstrates; Hezekiah refers to "my songs" (Isa. 38:20) that formed part of the temple liturgy (though some translations correct the Hebrew text to read "our stringed instruments"); there are fifteen psalms corresponding to the fifteen years' extension to his life; Hezekiah may indeed have written the ten anonymous songs, matching the ten degrees that the sundial receded, with the remaining five being chosen from the royal collection; and the contents of these psalms appear to approximate the circumstances of the triple crisis of Hezekiah's day: the Assyrian invasion, the king's desperate illness, and the lack of an heir to fill the throne. Indeed, the Hebrew word for "steps" could be, and was, translated "degrees." The only "degrees" Scripture informs us about were those mentioned in 2 Kings 20:8–11 (and its parallel in

Isa. 38:8). Accordingly, a fairly consistent case can be raised for Hezekiah's being the author of ten of these fifteen psalms with the background of the psalms alluding to events that were contemporaneous with Hezekiah.

According to this analysis, the fifteen psalms fall into five triads, each triad covering the triple experience of trouble, trust, and triumph, or distress, dependence, and deliverance, according to Arthur G. Clarke. The central psalm in the group would be 127, which is ascribed to Solomon, and each of the two sevens separated by this Solomonic psalm would contain two by David and five anonymous ones, which could then be attributed to Hezekiah. Contenders for this view also point out that each of the five triads ends or has as its theme for the psalm blessing or peace, reminding us of Hezekiah's last recorded words in 2 Kings 20:19—"'The word of the LORD you have spoken is good,' Hezekiah replied. For he thought, 'Will there not be peace and security in my lifetime?'"

There does appear to be some type of grouping and sequencing within the fifteen psalms. Many scholars group the first three psalms, as does the Hezekiah theory, and call them individual psalms that may well have functioned as solos. The next three or four psalms are communal in nature (123–126) and generally take the form of complaints offered to God. Almost everyone notes that psalms 127 and 128 are a pair. The next three psalms (129–131) introduce the note of hope, and function as communal psalms of confidence. Psalm 132 is a royal psalm offering the hope of a Messiah, while the last two psalms (133 and 134) sing the song of Zion and call the community to praise and benediction.

It is clear that these fifteen psalms contain elements that pick up almost all of the features that one or another of the already mentioned theories have focused on. Clearly the psalms do highlight the informing theology of the Aaronic benediction. They do mirror the progress of the pilgrim approaching and finally entering Jerusalem on each of the three annual feasts. And it may well be that Hezekiah's experiences did indeed form the background for the original setting of ten of these psalms, with Solomon contributing the central one and David four others, but with each of these last five being reappropriated under the inspiration of God to express Hezekiah's prayer and worship during his times of need and deliverance. If this indeed is the pattern, it may well guide us in reapplying these same truths to our contemporary scene. What would be more typical of Scripture than for it to function in just this way: that which was located in space and time again takes up the same principles in times of need and deliverance for modern men and women?

Psalms 120–134 make up a mere 10 percent of all the psalms in the Psalter. Their 101 verses constitute only 4 percent of the total number of verses in the whole book, yet there is an integrity and a wholeness to this collection that is bracketed by the longest psalm (119), with its acrostic form, and by the typical benediction of Psalm 134, usually used to signify the end of a collection in the Psalter (cf. Pss. 41:13; 72:19; 89:52; 106:48).

Throughout the generations interpreters have posited a logic and a development in these fifteen psalms that envisages a continuity based on the pilgrimage to Jerusalem. Typically the sequence is as follows:

120: The start from home with concern over what gossiping tongues will say; a weariness with the pagan environment

121: The first glimpse of the mountains of Zion; gratitude for the protection of Yahweh along the way

122: A song sung as the pilgrims pass into the gates of Jerusalem

123: A prayer of thanksgiving for mercy shown along the way and for grace to bear scorn, ridicule, and contempt

124: A song of thanksgiving for deliverance from peril

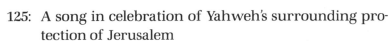

125: A song in celebration of Yahweh's surrounding protection of Jerusalem

126: The happy talk between the pilgrims and their hosts as they reflect on the great things God has done for them

127: A testimony that men and women are not the masters of their own fate, but all that takes place in life comes from the hand of God

128: A greeting and benediction for all the citizens of Jerusalem who came out to meet the pilgrims

129: A prayer for the enduring security of Jerusalem and a prayer for the vanquishing of all who hate Zion

130: A cry for forgiveness from the presence of God in the city where the presence of God dwells

131: A psalm of worship that celebrates the wisdom of adopting a lowly spirit in the presence of God and his works

132: A hymn celebrating the centrality of David and the promise God gave to him

133: An emotional outburst at the sight of the ministering priests in the house of God

134: A farewell benediction as the pilgrims prepare to leave for home and bless God's ministering servants in the twilight hours

While there is scanty support for such a detailed outline, some of the psalms seem to supply more evidence for such an interpretation than do others. A different logical order for these psalms was proposed by Evode Beaucamp, who sees a threefold recurrence of the ascent from anguish to total confidence in the Lord: Psalms 120–122, 123–128, 129–134. The focal point of all three is Jerusalem. In the first, one goes up to the city; in the second, one enjoys its security; and in the third, one gathers from Jerusalem guarantees for the future.

Note, however, how similar Beaucamp's outline is to the general one posed above.

Nevertheless, these psalms were written for the edification of the whole body of believers in all parts of the world and in all times. The best way to appreciate the teaching and theology of these fifteen psalms is to begin with the central psalm in the collection, Psalm 127. This is the psalm that was used by Luther, along with its twin, Psalm 128, to revolutionize family and social patterns during the Reformation. It is from Psalm 127 that we will be able to gain an abiding and a central focal point of reference for our study of this magnificent, but brief, collection. It is a veritable statement on the worthwhileness and wholesomeness of life in the home, the marketplace, and the nation. From this standpoint, the pilgrim can learn how to manage life and all its relations.

❖ **1** ❖

When They Spread Lies about You

Slander during the Journey

In October 1989, the city of Boston, Massachusetts, was pushed practically to the edge of racial riots when an outraged public believed the slanderous accusation of Charles Stuart. But the gripping tale of a couple shot by an African-American man on their way home from a childbirth class took a bizarre turn when the husband, who had survived a gunshot wound, suddenly jumped to his death from the Torbin Bridge into the Boston Harbor. Carol Stuart, thirty years of age and seven months pregnant, died the night of October 23 after having been shot in the head by her husband, Charles, it was later discovered. The story about the Stuarts' car having been commandeered by an African-American gunman was not true. Even more startling was the disclosure that some of Charles's family had also been involved in the plan to deceive the police, to frustrate justice, and to pin the guilt on someone else. It was Matthew Stuart who finally came forward in January 1990 to say that his brother Charles had asked him to be near the site where the murder took place. It was Charles who had handed Matthew a bag containing a snub-nose revolver, a Gucci handbag, a wallet, a makeup kit, and an engagement ring. But it was Matthew who disposed of these items in the Pines River, from which several of the items were almost immediately recovered.

Slander is a lethal weapon and can be used to destroy another person almost as effectively as can a revolver. In Psalm 120, pilgrims cannot help wondering, as they leave home for the religious celebrations in Jerusalem, whether they will be victims of a vicious smear campaign.

This psalm, then, is a prayer against lying lips. It is a prayer that that unruly member, the tongue, which can set the whole realm of nature on fire, might be restrained by the Lord of all history and providence.

Scripture often refers to this problem. For example, Jeremiah (9:8) warns,

> "Their tongue is a deadly arrow;
> it speaks with deceit.
> With his mouth each speaks cordially to his neighbor,
> but in his heart he sets a trap for him."

In the New Testament James likewise teaches, "The tongue is a fire, a world of evil among the parts of the body. It corrupts the whole person, sets the whole course of [one's] life on fire and is itself set on fire by hell" (3:6).

But why is this subject put first in this collection of pilgrim psalms? Samuel Cox, in his magisterial exposition of these psalms (*The Pilgrim Psalms: An Exposition of the Songs of Degrees*, London: R. D. Dickinson, 1885), answers our inquiry most fully when he concluded: "It is hardly an exaggeration to say that half of the miseries of human life spring from the reckless and malignant use of the tongue. And these wicked tongues generally wag fastest *behind a (person's) back, and amid the excitement of social intercourse.* We judge these sins of the tongue all too lightly, until we ourselves are injured by them" (p. 17, emphasis his). He continued, "As they left their homes for days or weeks together, would they not feel that they left their reputation at the mercy of their neighbors; that in their absence, behind their backs, words might be spoken, false words, the ill effects of which they could never undo? Would they not also feel that in the gossip of the caravan . . . they themselves might be tempted to speak unadvisedly, bitterly, untruly, with their lips—might yield to the temptation, and say words they would rue for many a day to come?" (p. 18).

Therefore it became exceedingly important that pilgrims would begin the journey to the festivals in Jerusalem with a prayer to be delivered from both the personal temptation to indulge in the wicked act of lying and slandering their neighbors, and the results of others' lying and slandering.

The psalm also carries a deep longing for peace. What a joyous release to be free from the babble of voices both from within and from without. Unfortunately, and all too frequently, such is the case in the marketplace: there are rivalries, emulations, contentions, and false rumors spread about by those with whom we work or who are our main competitors. Such is also the case in politics: what a wave of contradictory claims, bitter enmities, countercharges, and whisperings about what one or another has as a visible or a hidden agenda.

But is it any different in the home or in the church? Lying and slander also affect the home just as badly. There we find selfishness and jealousies that give way to all sorts of exasperating rumors, which can in turn result in spoiled relationships for years on end. Not even in the house of God can one always find a respite. Without distinction the lying tongue follows the worshiper and hinders even the most saintly efforts to see God's work prosper. No wonder the psalmist prays, in effect, "God of Peace: Let me get out of all of that—at least for the time that I draw apart to worship your name! Grant me a quiet sanctuary and asylum as I enter into your house and as I try to forget all the ill will, rancor, and strife that my enemies have so falsely raised against me."

Yes, there is a hiding place. We can be lifted above the nagging anxieties and the cacophony of a deceitful marketplace. The God of peace grants his peace to every restless, anxious heart that wants to rest. The living God alone is a match for all who seek to destroy tranquility of mind and reputation.

The psalmist was instructed by divine inspiration to lift up three pleas in Psalm 120. We are led, in these three pleas, from petition (vv. 1–2), to confidence (vv. 3–4), and lament (vv. 5–7).

Our Cry for Help (Ps. 120:1–2)

The pilgrim calls out to the Lord when setting out on the journey. The perfect verb in the Hebrew text is used in a present and continuing sense here: "I have often called and am still doing so." Thus begins the first of the Psalms of Ascent.

The petitioner feels as if there is some sort of confinement, for the word *distress* is the opposite of *being in a large room*. Space has "closed in" on the traveler, restricting and constricting.

The reason for this constricted feeling of distress is quickly supplied in verse 2: "lying lips." All of us have been victims of such misrepresentation. We tend to cower when attacked with lies. We are often left dispirited and feeling as if we have been ineffective and useless in what we have attempted to do.

But the Lord who said, "I am ... the truth" is the same Lord who also warned in the ninth commandment, "You shall not give false testimony" (Exod. 20:16). Isn't it refreshing to note how attention to God's word can embolden us in times just like those described in this psalm? God's promise came to the pilgrim's mind and therefore a cry went up to God in a time of deep distress. Let it be noted, however, that "liars and culminators are the most injurious people in the world, and yet they injure one as much as they do themselves; for they are accursed and an abomination to God—the Kingdom of the Devil is a Kingdom of lies ... but Christ's Kingdom is one of eternal truth" (Starke in *Lange's Commentary: The Psalms*, ed. Carl B. Moll [New York: Scribner, Armstrong, and Co., 1872], p. 605).

Only God can save us from the devastating effects of lies and slanderous talk. Our cry, therefore, is that the Lord deliver us from all lying lips and deceitful tongues. Few defense lawyers can make a case for our innocence and turn the evidence around to fit the guilty as can our Lord. He often makes the lie boomerang on those with whom it originated.

Our Confidence That God Will Respond (Ps. 120:3–4)

The three most common ways in which the tongue is employed as a weapon, according to Psalm 10:7, are through curses, lies, and threats. In fact, the tongue is one of the most frequently used weapons against the psalmist and all those whom he represents before God. "Not a word from their mouth can be trusted," he warns in Psalm 5:9. The tongues [of these liars and slanderers] are sharp swords," he cautions in Psalm 57:4. (See also Ps. 45:5.)

When the tongue has shot its deadly poisonous arrows of lies and slander (v. 3), what can we expect will happen? God's answer follows immediately in verse 4. God punishes those who launch the offensive with their own weapons—sharp arrows.

The burning coals of the broom tree are used figuratively here to express God's judgment on and punishment of all who defiantly abuse the gift of truth. It is said that the root of the broom tree yields a charcoal that retains its heat for a long time. Legend has it that travelers who, having cooked their food on a fire made from these roots, and having returned to the same spot a year afterward, found the embers still alive! A similar thing happens in punishment. Whereas the arrows of untruth are shot forth in an instant, the arrows of God's punishment on all who thoughtlessly steal the good reputations and worth of their neighbors will last for a long time.

For those who blacken others' character there is the unpleasant surprise that God eventually punishes them. Divine judgment may not be immediate, but it will come. As the poet said,

> Though the mills of God grind slowly,
>   yet they grind exceedingly small;
> Though with patience He stands waiting,
>   with exactness grinds He all.
> —Henry Wadsworth Longfellow, *Retribution*

Our Quest for Peace (Ps. 120:5–7)

At this point the psalmist lets out a deep sigh and we all join with him, for the truth of the matter is that we are left with a sad feeling of alienation and estrangement in circumstances such as these. Lies and slander leave us with a sense of loneliness and a sense of being cut off from friends and society. We are left to wonder what people will think and, worse yet, believe, if they hear such awful things being said about us.

For the pilgrims to endure such nonsense was tanta-mount to their dwelling among barbarians. The psalmist illustrates by singling out the most distant peoples of his world. To the north, these were the people of Meshech, who lived along the Caspian and Black seas. To the south this meant Kedar, where the people were descended from the second son of Ishmael (Gen. 25:13) and lived in black tents. Perhaps they were fiercely and implacably cruel in their day and thus they earned a double reason for being included in the thoughts of the psalmist at this point. But one thing is clear: the pilgrim felt out of place among a people that did not know God—the northerners being noted for their mili-tary might and the southerners for their trading ability. Too long had the pilgrim suffered calumnies at the hand of such people.

Have you ever been at the point where you wondered, "What on earth am I doing here? Why do I have to put up with all these false charges? I don't need all this trouble."

In such times we are tempted to respond in one of two ways. The first is to take the position of privatization, which says "I've had it and I'm not even going to answer these lies." The second is to take the position of compromise, sacrific-ing the truth for a quick fix to the damage that has been done. But God calls us to love the truth and to respond only with the truth, instead of allowing instinct to take over to the point where we strike back and use the weapon of lies and slan-der against those who have so badly damaged us. We begin to wonder if God will ever respond in our favor. We think that perhaps he is too occupied with matters of greater importance than to vindicate us and, because of this wrong thinking, we are tempted to take matters into our own hands.

The psalmist urges us to pursue peace, not hostilities. We are to be people of peace (v. 7). Our detractors are people of war; when they speak, it is to start a fight. But when we are smarting under the whip of another person's malicious tongue, we are to entreat God to deliver us and are not to take matters into our own hands.

Spurgeon once remarked, "A lie can go around the world while truth is putting on her boots" (from R. E. O. White, *You Can Say That Again* [Grand Rapids: Zondervan, 1991], 317). Yes, few things are as vicious and as unfair as a smear campaign constructed out of half-truths and lies. But our appeal must be made directly to our Lord and we must wait for his vindication if we are to be persons of peace.

Conclusion

What can a believer do in the face of slander and lies? The most obvious answer comes to us from 1 Peter 2:23. "When they hurled their insults at him, he did not retaliate; when he suffered, he made no threats. Instead he entrusted himself to him who judges justly." Moreover, "if you suffer for doing good and you endure it, this is commendable before God" (1 Pet. 2:20).

The way to do this is: "Do not repay evil with evil or insult with insult, but with blessing, because to this you were called so that you may inherit a blessing" (1 Pet. 3:9). In like manner our Lord taught in the Sermon on the Mount, "Blessed are you when people insult you, persecute you and falsely say all kinds of evil against you because of me. Rejoice and be glad, because great is your reward in heaven, for in the same way they persecuted the prophets who were before you" (Matt. 5:11–12).

Let us call on our Lord in times of distress, for he alone will certainly deliver us out of all the nets of falsehood and deceit. All our attempts to answer in kind or to extricate ourselves may only entangle us more deeply in the same type of nonsense that we despise so fiercely. Let us be men and women of peace and purpose in our own hearts—to speak only the truth and to resist with all our might and main error, falsehood, slander, and half-truths. Our God is the truth, speaks the truth, and demands the truth in every aspect of life. All those falling short of the truth must ultimately deal with him, not with us. Therefore, let us love the truth and hold fast to it in every aspect of life, whether in the marketplace, the judge's bench, the town hall, the home, or the church.

Questions for Thought and Discussion

1. Should I try to correct false statements when I have been lied about or slandered by others or should I leave it to God to act on my behalf? What attitude should I have toward the offenders? Would a lie be sufficient grounds for discontinuing fellowship?
2. Is Samuel Cox exaggerating when he writes that half of our human miseries are the result of the reckless and malicious use of the tongue?
3. Should we pray that we should escape the vicious results of a slanderous and lying tongue even before we are the known victims of such brutality? If we agree with that view, what form would such a prayer request take?
4. Is the announcement that God will, in effect, aim the arrows of the wicked back on themselves and punish them an indication that this is an Old Testament solution and not the gracious response of the loving God of the New Testament? Is this a form of taking the law into our own hands?
5. If God and all that he stands for is so right and so powerful, why do the effects of lies get around the world while truth is just putting on its boots? Or don't lies have such devastating effects? Does it just seem that way?

Psalm 120

Isaac Watts   (C.M.)

Thou God of love, Thou ever-blest,
   Pity my suff'ring state;
When wilt Thou set my soul at rest
   From lips that love deceit?

Peace is the blessing that I seek,
   How lovely are its charms!
I am for peace; but when I speak,
   They all declare for arms.

New passions still their souls engage,
   And keep their malice strong:
What shall be done to curb thy rage,
   O thou devouring tongue!

Should burning arrows smite thee through,
   Strict justice would approve;
But I had rather spare my foe,
   And melt his heart with love.

❖ 2 ❖

When Your Life Is Threatened

Danger during the Journey

Security! It is almost a modern mania—probably because there is so little real sense of being safe. As a result some have made our insecurities the basis for many a modern industry.

"We will protect you," the advertisements cry. "Have your insecurities met by our plan to protect you from every eventuality." Accordingly, we find ourselves purchasing flight insurance, depositing money into IRAs, taking advantage of tax shelters, joining health clubs, and trying to find a thousand and one solutions to whatever might befall us.

My wife and I will not soon forget the experience we had in the old city of Jerusalem one Friday afternoon in 1980. The Muslim feast of Ramadan (days of rigid fasting from dawn to sunset) had concluded when unexpectedly thousands of stirred-up worshipers poured from the mosque on the dome of the rock. We had been peacefully browsing through the shops on the narrow streets, called *suks*, just prior to being surrounded by hordes of Arabs who were evidently in a belligerent mood. Suddenly right in front of us and just short of the exit near the Damascus Gate a fight broke out. Everyone, Muslim worshiper, resident, and tourist were being pressed body to body. The crowd was beginning to panic. Suddenly, without warning, a dark-skinned man in a uniform, whom neither of us could identify then or clearly remember now, gestured to us from a very narrow opening in an alleyway and said, "You people are in trouble. Come! Follow me. You must leave this area immediately." Somehow we broke loose from the crowd and found ourselves in the dark alley following this stranger. After a number of turns, we emerged onto a less crowded street and were instructed to leave the area without further delay.

We were puzzled. Had we seen an angel? Or was our rescuer an undercover Israeli agent looking out for the tourists? To this day we are unable to tell you for sure. But you will never convince us that we were not miraculously kept from harm.

That is the key theme of Psalm 121. Six times the psalmist repeats the idea that the Lord *keeps* us and that he is our helper.

No less than in our own day, when a pilgrim left home in that day, there were always concerns for safety along the way. But this psalm teaches us that God's providence and protection cover our entire lives and has extended over all time. The theme of this psalm is very similar to God's promise to Jacob as he left home for Paddan Aram, "I am with you and will watch over you wherever you go" (Gen. 28:15).

My friend Brian Morgan related how a mutual acquaintance, Pastor Dave Roper of Cole Community Church in Boise, Idaho, prayed with his wife as he was leaving on a trip,

"Dear Lord, please protect Carolyn and the children while I'm gone." When he finished, Carolyn looked up and said, "Who do you think protects us while you're here?" Precisely so! God's protection is so constant that we think of it only when we are faced with an emergency or a time of travel.

By contrast this wonderful psalm is the expression of the individual who rejoices in the fact that God is our keeper. In fact, the Keeper of Israel and the Maker of heaven and earth is also the Keeper of individuals and of all who call on him for help. The ever-recurring thought in this brief psalm is to be found in the repetition of the word *keep* (six times), and in the second person pronominal suffix *you* (ten times), and in the use of the word *Lord* as the subject (ten times).

The eight verses of the psalm seem to be arranged so as to answer four questions for every two verses:

Who is our Keeper? (vv. 1–2)
How close is our Keeper to us? (vv. 3–4)
From what does our Keeper protect us? (vv. 5–6)
What are the limits of our Keeper's vigilance? (vv. 7–8)

One may even notice the special artistry that binds this psalm together. For example, verse 1 ends with "my help" while verse 2 begins with the same expression. Verse 3 ends with "he who watches over you will not slumber" and verse 4 begins with "he who watches over Israel will not slumber." Likewise verses 7 and 8 are linked by the same literary device that is usually called a staircase parallelism: "The LORD ... will watch over your life" and "The LORD will watch over your coming and going." Each verse, then, treats this single motif: the assistance that can be expected from the LORD, who is maker of heaven and earth, for all who need his protection and safety on the journey ahead.

The writer does not indicate the exact time or place of this psalm. Many see the setting, as judged by its placement in this group of Psalms of Ascent, as being the pilgrims' approach to Jerusalem. Suddenly they detect in the distance the Judean hills and they yearn for an immediate arrival at the Holy City, Zion, Jerusalem. A few scholars, however, prefer instead to place this psalm in the context of the tradition of one's facing Jerusalem when one prays, as outlined in 1 Kings 8:44, 48 and in Daniel 6:9–12. Thus they place the psalmist in a faraway land, perhaps as one of the exiles, longing for the city of God. But there is nothing here to indicate that this psalm is distinctively exilic in its outlook or that it has the place and orientation of prayer as its basis. Preferable is the theory that the pilgrims were on the last leg of one of their triannual journeys up to the city of Jerusalem. At evening, as they made preparations for their last encampment, they beheld, far off on the horizon against the dying light of the western sky, the Holy City. That sight alone was enough to fill them with joy and thankfulness for God's providential guidance, protection, and safety. Perhaps one voice began: "I will lift up my eyes to the hills..." and another responded in song or in antiphonal response, "He will not let your foot slip," to which the whole company of pilgrims chorused, "Indeed, he who watches over Israel will neither slumber nor sleep."

Psalm 121 supplies us with at least three assurances:

the assurance of the source of our help (vv. 1–2)
the assurance of the certainty of our help (vv. 3–6)
the assurance of the limitlessness of our help (vv. 7–8)

The Assurance of the Source of Our Help (Ps. 121:1–2)

The hazards of travel in olden days were much different than they are today. For those in antiquity there were ravines to cross (bridges were seldom in place as they are in modern travel), broken bones and unexpected injuries to be avoided, wild beasts and robbers to be shunned, not to mention the possibility of sunstroke, physical fatigue, inadequate supplies of food and water, or the inordinate amount of time it took to travel even short distances.

Although our travel hazards are different today, such a list only raises the whole subject of the insecurities of life, whether they be physical, financial, psychological, or spiritual. To be overly concerned about any or all of these factors of everyday life can paralyze us. It is this kind of fear that can do more than just intimidate us—it can place us in mortal fear for our lives and leave us hostage to all the unexpectedness of life.

To safeguard against all such fears the psalmist advises us to lift up our eyes rather than be downcast. The hills (v. 1) were either those of Judah or the ridge on which Jerusalem and the temple were located. How natural it was for the pilgrims to expect help to be forthcoming from Zion. Help would come from God's sanctuary: from the Lord himself (Ps. 14:7; 20:3).

Accordingly, the questions for each of us are: "What is the connection for me?" "Where does my help come from?" Verse 2 supplies the answer. Our helper is none other than the "Maker of heaven and earth." The Creator of the universe is a personal helper to pilgrims on a journey! But that has always been the connection of Scripture. The omnipotent Creator (Gen. 1) is immediately connected with the personal God who walks and talks with Adam in the Garden of Eden (Gen. 2).

The title *Maker of heaven and earth*, which has found its way into creedal statements such as the Apostles' Creed, is found only here and in Psalms 115:15; 124:8; 134:3. In most of these places it shows the power of God in contrast to the impotency of the heathen gods. All who call on the living God have available one who had enough power and ability to create both the heavens in all their immensity and the earth with all its variety. That fact alone ought to be help enough for all who despair and who call out in their time of need.

The Assurance of the Certainty of Our Help (Ps. 121:3–6)

Even if there is no dispute about the enormity of the power of God, it will occur to many to ask, perhaps even to doubt, whether God will use his protecting power for little people like ourselves. To what extent will he go to help us?

First, the psalmist answers the question personally. He changes from the first person of verses 1–2 to the second person in verses 3–6 in order to instruct all of us. Accordingly, then (v. 3), we may be assured that not even our foot will slip or stumble. The psalmist uses this phrase as a figure of speech to denote any type of trouble or misfortune as he has said elsewhere:

> My steps have held to your paths;
>   my feet have not slipped (Ps. 17:5)

> For I said, "Do not let them gloat
>   or exalt themselves over me when my foot slips"
>   (Ps. 38:16)

> He has preserved our lives
>   and kept our feet from slipping (Ps. 66:9)

Our Lord will protect us even in the smallest and most idiosyncratic of problems—even when they appear to be too trite and too personal to bring before the high and holy God of the universe.

The psalmist continues in verse 3 to say that it cannot be said that our God sleeps or slumbers. This is said in order to make a sharp contrast between our God and other gods such as Baal (1 Kings 18:27). Elijah taunted the prophets of Baal: "Maybe [Baal] is sleeping and must be awakened." Baal could not be expected, if he were real at all, which he was not, to stay up day and night and to keep his eye on all that was going on—especially with the ordinary people! But our God does just that. Never is he afflicted with the need for rest.

Even those passages that appear to refute this claim, such as Psalm 44:23, "Awake, O LORD! Why do you sleep? Rouse yourself! Do not reject us forever," do not contradict it. The point is not that God has been napping, because the word *to awake* can also be translated *to arouse oneself.* Therefore, what is being asked in this psalm is that God accelerate his long-suffering patience and bring the required and expected justice to a speedy conclusion. We can conclude that the same God who has given safety, security, protection, and guidance to the whole nation of Israel will do the same for all who call on him.

Yes, "the LORD watches over you." Verse 5 repeats the verb variously translated "to guard," "to watch over," or "to keep." The LORD will be our "shade" against the burning rays of the sun. Those who abide under the shadow of the hand of God stand under his protection. Elsewhere the psalmist has equated God's protection with mortals hiding in the shadow of his wings (Ps. 17:8), with taking refuge in the shadow of his wings (Ps. 57:1), and with resting in the shadow of the Almighty (Ps. 91:1). Like the psalmist, Isaiah depicts God's protection as our being covered with the shadow of his hand (Isa. 51:16).

In fact, so all-encompassing is God's providence as represented by the hand and shade of God that he will protect us from anything that might come against us "by day . . . or by night." This figure of speech, called a merism because it embraces everything from one shore to the other, to use another merism, surely wants us to entrust everything that happens to us to his loving care—day or night.

Some pilgrims feared the heat of the day because of possible sunstroke. Others believed, whether rightly or wrongly (we will not say in this context), that lunacy, presumably from the injurious rays of the moon, could be a problem. The author of this psalm points out that regardless of the situation God will be our helper in every eventuality. The point is that God can protect in the day or the night.

Beyond this concern for protection from physical harm for self and loved ones there lies the reality of evil, which affects us as much as it did the pilgrim. Evil is often hidden to us, and from this we must also have God's protection. Whatever the situation we are assured that we will not stumble or slip over the precipice: our God will not be sleeping at precisely the moment we need him.

How many times have we been in harm's way and never knew it because our God had been watching over us day and night? So often, whether traveling by air, by auto, or merely as we have been walking along, we may have been exposed to danger only to have been silently, but most definitely, delivered by the God who never slumbers or sleeps.

The Assurance of the Limitlessness of Our Help (Ps. 121:7–8)

What, then, can separate us from the love of God? "Nothing," answers the psalmist. The loving evidence of God's protection can be seen all around us if we will only open our eyes.

Our Keeper watches us from the time we awake and go out into the often dangerous marketplace until we return home. Derek Kidner has written, "It would be hard to decide which half of [verse 8] is more encouraging, the fact that it starts 'from now,' or that it runs on, not to the end of time, but without end" (*Psalms 73–150: A Commentary on Books III–IV* [London: Inter-Varsity, 1977], 432). God's keeping power does not begin sometime in the future. We have it now. It continues into the future.

The Hebraic expression, "your coming and going" (v. 8), denotes all the circumstances and occupations of life. It includes everything—our trips away from home and back and the kids on their way to school and on their way home—no matter what, all day and night. What a fabulous Lord who continues to watch over so many in such minute detail that it is mind-boggling. Indeed, the Lord is our helper, keeper, and shade. Therefore we may confidently cast all our cares, concerns, and fears on him, because he cares for us.

Conclusion

Why do we load ourselves with so many burdens and fears? In these anxious and fearful days we must learn to cast our cares on him.

But how do we do this? It is one thing to say that God will protect us, but it is another thing to experience his protection. How can one not worry in these days of drunken drivers on the road, terrible plane crashes, terrorists who blow up airports, and who knows what else? How can we stop worrying about the rapists, the child molesters, and abusers of all ilks? Isn't it humanly foolish to walk around most metropolitan areas at night? How can we stop worrying about all of these things?

We can do much to lessen our anxiety when we dwell more on the loving goodness of God whose eyes never leave us or our children. We do much to lessen anxiety when we remember that he will never let our foot slip over the edge without personally being there with us and our loved ones. It is not as if we could say, as Martha said to the Lord when he arrived after her brother Lazarus had died, "Lord, if you had been here, my brother would not have died" (John 11:21). The point for us is that the Lord did come, he was there. And he will be there for us in every moment of life. That has to be worth more comfort than all the security systems and insurance policies we can buy.

God is our defender and shield. He is not a man to be thought of as growing weary or becoming exhausted, fatigued, or even distracted by major world events. Let us confess our insecurities. Let us pray to God to be released from our extra, unnecessary baggage of worry, fretting, and anxiety. Recall once again that the Lord is our helper, protector, and life. He will watch over us both now and forevermore—even on into eternity!

Questions for Thought and Discussion

1. How can a God who is so transcendent and so far above us be involved in the day-to-day activity of our daily lives? Isn't this a philosophical impossibility that pulls him in two different directions at the same time?
2. If God is the keeper of the nation of Israel, what can be said about the subject of God's providence regarding the other nations in antiquity and modernity? Did or does God also watch over them? If so, to what extent? What is our biblical reason for saying so?
3. What does Psalm 121 teach, if anything at all, about the possibility of the moon harming us? Does this text teach older views about the sources of lunacy?
4. If the Lord promises to protect us from all harm (v. 7), then how can we explain the fact that many believers and their loved ones experience evil and harm?
5. What part does daily prayer, lifting our eyes up to the hills, play in our release from the worry of anxiety? What part does prayer have in our fixing our hearts on the assurance guaranteed to us in this chapter?

Unto the Hills

John Campbell, 1845–1914   (Sandon 10. 4. 10. 4. 10. 10)

Unto the hills around do I lift up
My longing eyes;
O whence for me shall my salvation come,
From whence arise?
From God the Lord doeth come my certain aid,
From God the Lord who heav'n and earth hath made.

He will not suffer that thy foot be moved—
Safe shall thou be;
No careless slumber shall his eyelids close
Who keepeth thee.
Behold, he sleepeth not, he slumb'reth ne'er,
Who keepeth Israel in his holy care.

Jehovah is himself thy keeper true,
Thy changeless shade;
Jehovah thy defense on thy right hand
Himself hath made.
And thee no sun by day shall ever smite;
No moon shall harm thee in the silent night.

From every evil shall he keep thy soul,
From ev'ry sin;
Jehovah shall preserve thy going out,
Thy coming in.
Above thee watching, he whom we adore
Shall keep thee henceforth, yea, for evermore. Amen.

Psalm 121

Isaac Watts   (C.M.)

To heav'n I lift my waiting eyes,
   There all my hopes are laid:
The Lord that built the earth and skies
   Is my perpetual aid.

Their feet shall never slide to fall,
   Whom He designs to keep;
His ear attends the softest call,
   His eyes can never sleep.

He will sustain our weakest powers
   With his almighty arm,
And watch our most unguarded hours
   Against surprising harm.

Israel, rejoice and rest secure,
   Thy keeper is the Lord;

His wakeful eyes employ His power
   for Thine eternal guard.

Nor scorching sun, nor sickly moon
   Shall have his leave to smite;
He shields thy head from burning noon,
   From blasting damps at night.

He guards thy soul, He keeps thy breath
   Where thickest dangers come;
Go and return, secure from death,
   Till God commands thee home.

❖ 3 ❖

When Church Bores You

Worship during the Journey

Arrival! How sweet the sound of this word and its reality to the ears of the weary traveler. So often I have been in an airport waiting lounge and have witnessed one happy reunion after another as a husband, a wife, a father, or some other relative emerged from the door. There are few joys that compare to the enthusiasm of many of these greetings.

But how much more joyous was the arrival of the pilgrims, who after having traveled those many miles on foot over the Palestinian turf, were at last in the city of God, Jerusalem. This psalm, which is ascribed to King David, describes the pilgrims' emotions as they anticipated entering Jerusalem and the thrill of actually setting foot within the gates of the city of God. All were stirred to awe and wonder by the sight of the city—its walls, citadels, and inner courtyards. But the climax of all their emotions came when they finally reached the house of God itself, the place of the very presence of God.

Of all the pilgrim psalms from Psalm 120 to 134, this is *the* pilgrim psalm. Almost certainly it was originally written for the occasion when the festival-bound pilgrims drew near to and then finally entered the streets of Jerusalem and passed on to the temple. More than a child's anticipating Disneyland or a tourist's first glimpse of an exotic vacationland, the joy one experiences on entering the city of God has few, if any, real comparisons.

I shall never forget the first time I visited Jerusalem in the spring of 1980. We had traveled from Chicago to Rome with forty seminary students. From Rome we went on to Tel Aviv. The darkness had already set in as we boarded the bus that would take us from that seacoast international-airport town up the long, slow climb to Jerusalem. Finally at ten o'clock in the evening we rounded a corner and there lay the high wall of the old city on its western side near the Joppa gate. I could not believe my eyes: orange-tinted spotlights played on the ancient walls that stood thirty to forty feet high, interrupted only by the massive gates that lent an even more imposing impression. We had arrived at that famous city where God himself had dwelt in his enshrouding glory and where so much of the plan of our salvation had unfolded.

What do we mean, however, when we call Jerusalem the city of God? Surely it would be a mistake to connect a definition of this city merely with its stones, buildings, or even its people. Any biblical theology of the city is ultimately a theology of two cities: the city of man and the city of God.

It was this very city of Jerusalem that our Lord loved enough to weep over. He exclaimed, "O Jerusalem, Jerusalem, you who kill the prophets and stone those sent to you, how often I have longed to gather your children together, as a hen gathers her chicks under her wings, but you were not willing" (Matt. 23:37). The earthly city could not be divorced from its spiritual potential.

But what had made Jerusalem unique was the fact that it was the place where God had caused his name, his presence, and his glory to dwell. Accordingly, this city was the place where the worshiper could come before the presence of the living God, under the rule of David's offspring and the pledge of the Messiah who was to come, in order to fellowship with all the saints.

David may have first published this composition shortly after he removed the ark of the covenant to Zion (2 Sam. 6). David certainly encouraged the people to regard Jerusalem, not Gibeon where the sanctuary had been previously, as being the true center of worship. One need only recall how joyous an occasion it was for David and the people when the ark of the covenant was finally brought into the city of Jerusalem itself. David danced and leaped for joy (to the disdain of his wife Michal). Shortly after this episode, God made the most mind-boggling announcement: David's seed, house, and throne not only would carry on indefinitely, but also would be the very line, dynasty, and authority from which the Messiah himself would eventually come (2 Sam. 7). The affections of all Israel were drawn around this city and its sanctuary. There in Zion, the city of God, would lie God's affection.

Some have argued against a Davidic authorship of Psalm 122 because verses 4 and 5 use the historic present tenses for its verbs and thereby recall a later time when the tribes went up to Jerusalem. Because David had only recently won the city of Jerusalem away from the Jebusites, how, asked these challengers of the Davidic authorship, could David speak of this as being a place that had for generations past been the place to which the tribes resorted? In answer to this objection we point out that David personally experienced the joy of entering Jerusalem many times, yet that experience never became old or routine. But, regardless of the dating details, the delight in arriving at the city in any period must be acknowledged in this psalm.

In Praise of the City's Preeminence
(Ps. 122:1-5)

Years ago it was extremely common to enter a home and see a plaque on the wall that read, "I was glad when they said unto me, 'Let us go into the house of the Lord.'" And that is where this psalm begins. It begins with an invitation to enter the house of God. Few things can, and ought to, rejuvenate and refresh our spirits more than a trip to the house of God. Surely it did so for David and the pilgrims of those early days as they came into the city and into the court of the Lord.

The one who first spoke in the singular in verse 1 now speaks in verse 2 in the plural, "our feet." The journey now having been completed, the group stood within the gates of Jerusalem. The verb *stood* may be a strict perfect tense here; therefore it implied that long after the initial event they were in their mind's eye *still standing* there and continuing to savor the delight and satisfaction of mingling with the worshipers who crowded the court of God on those high holy days.

Two features of the city struck the pilgrims as they passed along its streets: first, how built up it was, and second, how compactly arranged everything was. When a peasant or a villager encountered for the first time the impressive density and the long rows of houses joined one to another, it had to have made a startling impression. After all, previous to this experience he or she had seen only poor and scattered dwellings with very little architectural finesse. They probably marveled over how closely joined together the buildings were and how well built and stately they were. The pilgrims' marveling was as great as was later the astonishment and wonderment of the disciples of Jesus as they sat one day on the Mount of Olives and exclaimed over the sheer beauty and magnificence of the temple mount. One can detect a note of surprise as the pilgrims gazed on this metropolis with more than a touch of pride and patriotic feeling.

But Jerusalem was also "closely compacted together." As soon as a visitor sees how the city conforms to the natural contours of the ground on which it stands, this exclamation can be better appreciated. The deep ravines that separate the city from the Mount of Olives to the east or from the ridges to the south and west made for excellent defense and for a natural counterpoint to everything around it. No matter how large the city might grow, it could not leap over the Valley of Kidron to the east or the Valley of Hinnon to the south. Moreover, the Tyropean Valley formed in earlier days a natural moat that shut Zion and Moriah into one compact mass. Consequently, every foot of ground was valuable. House was joined to house and every piece of exposed earth within the city walls was a potential paradise.

No wonder, then, the pilgrims recalled with joy the fact that they had responded to the summons, "Let us go to the house of the Lord." So impressed were they with the cityscape and with the fact that herein was the place where the Lord himself made his residence on earth that they could hardly contain their joy. There they were, *standing* in Jerusalem itself.

One wonders how deeply affected modern believers are by the opportunities that we have to enter along with other believers into the house of God. Do we find the suggestion to go to church a pleasant one? Are God's people the delight of our existence? Or do we find more excitement over the prospect of going out to the ballpark? Is being with the ungodly a more enjoyable prospect? A truthful answer to this question could tell us an amazing amount of information about ourselves and our relationship to the Lord and to his people.

There is a real need for a sense of community in our modern world, especially as we become more and more involved with technology. John Naisbitt, in his much-referred-to book *Megatrends*, describes one of the ten major trends affecting modern society as being one that he calls "hi-tech, hi-touch." In his estimation, the oftener modern society introduces technology into its life, the more people feel the need to congregate and to be together. One of Naisbitt's illustrations concerns the fact that many thought with the advent of VCRs, people would abandon the large public movie theaters in favor of viewing films in their own living rooms. However, most did not understand high-tech, high-touch. People go to a movie or other events in order to be with people—to laugh, to cry, or to cheer with hundreds or even thousands of other human beings. The more impersonal our society becomes through technology, the more people hunger for places in which to congregate and to be with others. This is true whether it is a crowded singles' bar, a movie, a rock concert, a shopping mall, or some other place where we can forget about our loneliness for a time.

What an opportunity for the church to reassert this ministry. Instead, the evangelical church has followed the route of high-tech rather than high-touch. The program of the church has collapsed at just the time when people are starving for friendship and company. Whereas the Sunday evening service once was one of the highlights of the week with many from nonevangelical churches attending to enjoy the unusually enriching singing, premier messages, and coffee time after the service at a local coffee shop, restaurant, or home, this ministry has all but dissolved in almost every evangelical church. Who among us now rejoices when we hear, "Let us go to the house of the Lord [on Sunday evening]?"

Verses 4 and 5 point even more definitively to the reasons for such outbursts of joy over the prospects of going to the house of God. Even then Jerusalem had already become the place to which all the tribes were beginning to resort. Because of the allusion to this historical fact, some feel that this psalm from David was reapplied to the time of the exile when enough time could have accumulated for the tribes to have been in the habit of going to Jerusalem. However, such a relocation in time may not be necessary; enough time had elapsed during David's own reign for all the tribes to begin such a habit. Nevertheless, nothing crucial hangs on this temporal decision, because either location in time fits.

Once the worshipers had arrived at the house of God, what were they to do? There is a great deal of discussion these days about modes of worship. Some prefer a contemporary service in which music is sung "off-the-wall" making use of an overhead projector, while others prefer a four-pound hymnbook and a more liturgical, formal type of worship. So what makes a service meaningful, worshipful, and honoring to our God?

Verses 4 and 5 suggest two purposes for worship. First, worship is a time when we give our praise to God, and second, worship is a time when we come under the judgment of God. Therefore, worship must feature a thankful heart and it must be accompanied with a humble and teachable spirit.

Three times each year all Israelite males were required to appear before the Lord (Exod. 23:17; 34:23; Deut. 16:16; cf. Ps. 81:3–5). Each of these appearances coincided with a feast that was related to one of the harvests in the agricultural cycle. The first was Passover, or the Feast of Unleavened Bread, which depicted our Lord's death. The second, the Feast of Pentecost, came fifty days later. It looked forward to the day when the Holy Spirit would be poured out on all believers. Later, in the fall, came the Feast of Tabernacles, or Booths, or Ingathering; it completed the agricultural cycle for the year. This feast anticipated the time when God would once again dwell in the midst of his people, made up of Jews and Gentiles (Zech. 14:16). All this was to be done "according to the statute given to Israel" (Ps. 122:4). The word *statute* contains the idea of "witness" and thus it had the flavor of being Israel's missionary call to reach out to the nations.

The worshipers came, therefore, to give thanks to God for the harvests and for all that he had meant to them in life. In each event they pointed forward to the rising of Christ from the dead, to the coming of the Holy Spirit, and to the time when all will dwell under the shadow of the physical presence of God in the midst of men and women on earth.

But worship is also a time for personal inspection and God's judging of our hearts. Just as the people in David's day brought their appeals for justice to the king's court in the royal city, so likewise the worshiper of today must be ready for the searching and inspecting work of the Holy Spirit in God's house. Jesus demonstrated this aspect of worship when he cleansed the temple on the first day of the feast. Later as he taught there he brought the attitude of the scribes and Pharisees under his scrutiny and judgment (Matt. 23).

Accordingly, when we come before the Lord's presence, we too come under the same judgment of the Spirit. Worship happens, not only when we lift our voices in praise of the living God, but also when we place ourselves under the inspection of the Word of God and respond to the conviction of the Holy Spirit.

In Prayer for the City's Peace (Ps. 122:6–9)

The main words in this strophe are peace and prosperity. The Hebrew word for peace is *shalom* and the word for prosperity is *shalvah*. Since Jerusalem is the city of peace (*Yeru-shalaim*), this psalm wishes *shalom* and *shalvah* on the very city so named.

No doubt this is the pilgrim's prayer for the city wherein the house of God was located. The predominant feature of peace is a sense of wholeness and a well-being that resulted from that wholeness. Prosperity connoted a tranquil and quiet spirit. One was able to relax and take his ease during prosperous times.

The psalmist calls on believers everywhere and in all ages to pray for the peace of Jerusalem—a city that has remained at the center of the program of God for such a long time. He wishes prosperity for all who love her and pray for her. He likewise wishes the same for all his brothers and friends, "Peace be within you" (v. 8).

As long as the house of God stands, it will be central to our affections and to our desires for effectiveness and completeness. The place of worship was held to be the center and the mainstay of the life of the nation of Israel—and so it should be everywhere. Given the fact that the house of God is the palace of the Most High, that house must be uppermost in our thoughts and actions.

Conclusion

The obvious pride and joy that the believing Hebrew had in worshiping God in the city where God had caused his name to dwell lies evident in this psalm. Even though contemporary Christians do not have a sacred city, or even a splendid temple, we do have the same Lord and the same fellowship to which he invited those of olden days.

Our father, like the father of the Hebrews, is also Abraham. Thus we share one Lord, one faith, and one baptism. We are members together of one body in Christ, the Messiah. By faith we also have been made to participate in the same fellowship of the body of Christ.

But we must also, in our day, feel the happy summons to his house. If those ancient believers could leave their homes thrice every year and expose themselves to the hazards of a perilous journey for a week of worship in the house of God, can we not also take the time for uninterrupted worship of the living God in his house? What sort of sacrifices have we made in order to minister to others? How often have we made attendance at the house of God a priority in our schedules, or is it more of a chore that we feel we must do or others will criticize us? How frequently have we been willing to let the word of God judge us, or do we turn off God's spokesperson when the message is too personal and condemnatory of things that we would rather not have exposed to the searching light of Scripture?

The psalmist searched for the good, the success of the house of God, and the prosperity of the city of God. Can we say as much for ourselves? And since God has by no means finished with his city of Jerusalem, can we say that we continue to pray for the peace of Jerusalem? Do we still long for the completion of the program of God as it centers in his house and in the ancient city of Zion? May it be so. Let us be glad when they say unto us, "Let us go to the house of the Lord."

Questions for Thought and Discussion

1. Have you ever taken a trip to Jerusalem? If so, what were your feelings as you viewed the city where our Lord walked? If not, how do you picture the city?
2. How central do you think the city of Jerusalem is to the plan of God as he concludes history? What passages

come to your mind from Scripture that are relevant to this thesis?

3. In what ways are you fulfilling your need for high-touch in our high-tech society? Could the church more adequately fulfill these needs for you as presently programmed or as modified?

4. If the worship service were your responsibility, which features would you include and which ones would you drop? If worship includes adoration, confession, thanksgiving, supplication, and fellowship, how do the two features of praise and judgment in this psalm fit that description?

5. What responsibility do contemporary Christians have to pray for the peace of Jerusalem without becoming so partial to the Israeli cause that we err on the side of being unsympathetic to the cause of Palestinian Arabs, both Christians and non-Christians?

Psalm 122

Isaac Watts   (C.M.)

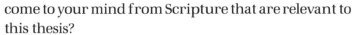

How did my heart rejoice to hear
    My friends devoutly say,
In Zion let us all appear,
    And keep the solemn day!

I love her gates, I love the road;
    The place adorned with grace
Stands like a palace built for God
    to show His milder face.

He hears our praises and complaints;
    And while His awesome voice
Divides the sinners from the saints,
    We tremble and rejoice.

Peace be within this sacred place,
And joy a constant guest!
With holy gifts and heav'nly grace
Be her attendants blest!

My soul shall pray for Zion still,
While life or breath remains;
There my best friends, my kindred dwell,
There God my Saviour reigns.

❖ 4 ❖

When Others Treat You Unfairly

Suffering during the Journey

Several years ago the whole nation was stunned by the testimony of a woman who claimed that as a born-again Christian she felt obligated to confess a wrong she had perpetrated almost a dozen years previously. She had falsely accused a man of raping her, and he had been sent to prison for that crime. However, she knew that her lie had resulted in the incarceration of an innocent man. She wanted to recant. Ultimately, the convicted man was set free, but what a long time he had had to wait for vindication and for freedom.

Psalms 123 and 124 exhibit the same longing for release, though the Lord is the vindicator rather than the revised testimony of an accuser or the decision of a court.

The setting for these psalms has been disputed. Because Psalm 124 is attributed to David in the title line (a line that has not been thought to be part of the inspired text by most Bible scholars), the time for its writing has been thought to have been during David's wars with the Syrians and Edomites, or more preferably during the time when David was being pursued by Saul (1 Sam. 23–26). This later setting certainly fits well with the anguish expressed here (especially since I tend to regard these psalm titles as part of the inspired text, contrary to the majority opinion of most Bible teachers).

But it is also clear that many of these texts, particularly the psalms, were used by later generations when they too were in similar circumstances, just as we tend to do in our day. Accordingly, it may well be that King Hezekiah, or one of the inspired prophets of his day, took an earlier psalm by David and revised it slightly for use in the national emergency that arose under the attempted Assyrian invasion (ca. 700 B.C.). The contemptuous field commander of the Assyrian king Sennacherib shouted to the people on the wall of Jerusalem, "'This is what the great king, the king of Assyria, says: On what are you basing this confidence of yours?...And if you say to me, "We are depending on the LORD our God"—isn't he the one whose high places and altars Hezekiah removed, saying to Judah and Jerusalem, "You must worship before this altar"?... "Do not let Hezekiah mislead you when he says, 'The LORD will deliver us.' Has the god of any nation ever delivered his land form the hand of the king of Assyria?... How then can the LORD deliver Jerusalem from my hand?" (Isa. 36:4–20).

What is most uncanny about the suggestion of this historical allusion as the basis for these two psalms is the fact that according to the famous Sennacherib Cylinder (now in the British Museum), the Assyrian king boasts that he shut up Hezekiah like a bird in a cage. There is a strong possibility that the reference to Judah's escape "like a bird out of the fowler's snare" in Psalm 124:7 reflects Hezekiah's deliverance after Sennacherib had boasted to the contrary. Indeed, God sent Hezekiah relief and 185,000 soldiers lost their lives in one night before the Assyrian king suddenly broke off his siege of Jerusalem and slipped out of the country (2 Kings 18–19). One ancient writer attributed the deliverance to mice and rats that ate the strings of the Assyrians' bows. This scenario has led many moderns to conjecture that the bubonic plague broke out suddenly and that that is how God sent his deliverance. Nevertheless, no matter how Jerusalem was delivered, a deliverance it certainly was!

The most venerable set of messages ever delivered on these passages were composed by Samuel Cox in 1885. He places these psalms in the postexilic period, after the return of Judah from the Babylonian captivity. Even though Cox agrees that Psalm 123 contains no clear indication of its date or authorship, he feels that the period after the return of Ezra and Nehemiah is the time frame that best matches the known events. It was after the exile that the local inhabitants of Palestine heaped scorn and contempt on Judah. Especially disheartening were the speeches of Sanballat, Tobiah, and Geshem: "What is this you are doing? . . . Are you rebelling against the king?" (Neh. 2:19). "What are those feeble Jews doing? Will they restore their wall? . . . Will they finish in a day? . . . What they are building—if even a fox climbed up on it, he would break down their wall of stones!" (Neh. 4:2–3). The most that Nehemiah could do was to pray, "Hear us, O our God, for we are despised. Turn their insults back on their own heads" (Neh. 4:4).

Indeed, the vocabulary and style of Psalm 123 easily fit David, but several of the phrases are uniquely suited to Hezekiah. Therefore, this was most likely a Davidic psalm that the Spirit of God had someone in Hezekiah's day adapt. Psalm 123 became part of the pilgrims' repertoire as they journeyed to the temple, and then it became part of our Scripture under the instruction of the Holy Spirit.

Cox's praise of Psalm 123 is effusive:

This Psalm has one distinction which is to be found in "scarcely any other piece in the Old Testament." In the Hebrew, it has rhymes.... [But it is also] perfect as it stands. It is a little gem, cut with the most exquisite art. Few poems, inspired or uninspired, have been more admired or beloved. It has the charm of unity. It limits itself to one thought; or rather, it expresses a single mood of the soul—the upward glance of a patient and hopeful faith. Hence it has been well called *Oculus Speceans*, the "Eye of Hope." This unity moreover, is blended with and enhanced by variety of expression. While the first strophe sounds and illustrates the single theme of the Psalm, the second, to use a musical term, is a "variation" upon it. [*The Pilgrim Psalms*, 68-70]

Our Watching for God's Gracious Vindication (Ps. 123:1–2)

The psalmist, acting on our behalf "till he shows his mercy" (v. 2), lifts his eyes to God whose throne is in heaven and fixes his eye on the hand of God. He then awaits some sign, some signal, some gesture, however slight, that will indicate what the Lord's will is. The psalmist likens himself a domestic or household servant waiting to anticipate, if possible, any wish of master or mistress, even if expressed only by a slight movement of a finger or a nod of the head with a shift of the eyes. The slave in this case is a picture of the suppliant who waits in prayer for the slightest indication as to how his or her master will respond.

The opening words of Psalm 123 are very similar to those of Psalm 121—"I lift up my eyes to the hills." Here, however, the psalmist goes beyond the hills to heaven itself.

Verses 1 and 2 are arranged in a chiasmus (a reversal of the order of words in two or more parallel lines). Translated literally and in the original order of the Hebrew text, they read:

A. To you I raise my eyes, O Enthroned One in heaven,
  B. Behold, as the eyes of servants are
    toward the hand of their lords
  B. As the eyes of the maid are
    toward the hand of her mistress
A. So our eyes are toward the LORD our God
  until he shows us his graciousness.

Thus verse 1 begins with proposition A and verse 2 ends with proposition A' with comparisons B and B' situated between the two propositions. Note also that the first and fourth lines refer to the Lord while the middle two refer to humans. Lines 1 and 4 have the first person pronoun while lines 2 and 3 are in the third person.

The fact that a broader, universal truth is referred to can be seen from the fact that verse 2 ends with the benefits coming to all of us. The psalmist is the representative of all who can name the Lord as "our God." Those who have suffered the biting remarks, insults, ignominy, shame, and verbal assaults of oppressors will long for any indication of God's gracious intervention on their behalf.

Over the years Israel faced the taunts and scorn of the Syrians, the Assyrians, the Babylonians, the Greeks, and the Romans. Again and again they had to take refuge in the fact that he who sat enthroned in heaven could see their plight and would graciously defend them when they were contemptuously challenged.

The remainder of these past deliverances only made the pilgrims, as they thought on these things, all the more resolute in their longing to see the vindicating, powerful hand of God move once again. Even more startling is the thought of Jesus' traveling along the same route centuries later. For twenty years of his life, he too must have made many of these annual trips up to Jerusalem from Galilee. This pilgrim song book must have been on his lips as well. His mood may well have reflected the words of Isaiah, which depict what Christ would go through in order to obtain our salvation. "He was despised and rejected of men . . . he was oppressed and afflicted . . . a man of sorrows and acquainted with grief, . . . yet we esteemed him not" (53:3). Would our Lord Jesus not cry out all the more knowingly, "I will lift up my eyes to you whose throne is in heaven"? He too must have expressed his utter dependence on the Father and waited with that same patient trust with which we must also wait.

Our Prayer for God's Gracious Relief
(Ps. 123:3–4)

The second strophe takes up the theme of verses 1 and 2 and expands them in verses 3 and 4 with a slight variation of the same hope. Here the suppliant breaks out into a *kyrie eleison*, "Have mercy on us, O LORD." We shift our focus from the eyes of the suppliant to the prayer on his lips.

The earnestness of this prayer warrior may be deduced from the fact that the request, "be gracious" or "have mercy," is repeated three times in a row (the end of verse 2 and the beginning of verse 3). Moreover, the extent to which the suppliant has suffered may be gauged from other repetitions: "for we have endured much contempt," "we have endured much ridicule from the proud," "much contempt from the arrogant" (vv. 3–4).

The poet is clear that the despised ones were weary with all this verbal abuse. Literally, "we are fully sated with contempt, fully sated is our soul with ridicule from the proud" (vv. 3b–4).

There the matter stands. No words of resentment or impatience accompany this psalm. The suppliant asks only for God's intervention and for God's grace in the face of being wronged. Surely God will show his mercy.

Our Thanksgiving for God's Gracious Deliverance (Ps. 124:1–5)

The first five verses of this psalm are held together by a series of logical propositions. Each one clearly marked by the opening words *had it not been* (vv. 1, 2) and *then/therefore* (vv. 3, 4, 5). Thus the artistry of this first strophe is such that it presents a condition in verse 1, expands on it in verse 2, and then offers a consequence in verse 3, a second consequence in verse 4, and a third consequence in verse 5.

The psalmist sings, "If there had ever been a time when we had almost lost it and when we had almost gone over the edge, these were the times." The enemies are variously depicted in these verses. In verses 3 and 6 the enemies are likened to ravenous beasts that could swallow prey alive. In the intervening verses (vv. 4 and 5) the enemies are likened to raging waters and a torrent of water. Once again we see another type of chiasmus in this psalm. The Jewish population, without God's protection, would have been devoured like prey or would have been swept away by torrents of raging water. The Hebrew poetry adds phrase upon phrase in order to increase the impression made on the mind. Together these phrases embellish the horror and prolong an image of oppression.

But God was at their side. He was there when evil men attacked them. He was there when beastly enemies were ready to rip them apart with their anger. He was there when man's anger threatened to sweep them away like a flood.

Our Praise for God's Gracious Help (Ps. 124:6–8)

Verse 6 begins by invoking the name of the Lord, thereby echoing verses 1 and 2. In this manner, an envelope is formed around the triple announcement of what could have happened to Israel had not the Lord been present to deliver her (Daniel Grossberg, *Centripetal and Centrifugal Structures in Biblical Hebrew* [Atlanta: Scholars, 1989], 37).

Israel had escaped the teeth, fangs, and claws of her attackers because the Lord had been on her side. He disengaged the trap that had been set for them. They had escaped like birds who had swerved just in time to avoid the net as it was swinging up to capture them. One can almost hear the laugh of exaltation over defrauding the enemy of the pleasure of capturing them. It was a triumphant giggle of joy that comes in reaction to prolonged stress and then sudden relief.

Truly, the whole psalm is alive with joy, wonderment, and relief. But it is not the relief that boasts in one's own wit or prowess in bringing about that release; it is a joy that glories in God alone.

The psalm closes with a solemn ascription of praise to God. "Our help is in the name of the LORD, the Maker of heaven and earth" (v. 8). Because God made all things and is currently ruling over all that he made, is it any wonder that those crying out for deliverance can realize such wonderful rescues? Only such hope could, then as well as now, match any desperate situation that would send one to God for help. This was the secret to their confidence: a complete trust in God. He was able to deliver from each and every snare on the earth. He had already plucked many a hurting, drowning, besieged individual from the jaws of death, torment, and suffering. God could once again give them rest from all their enemies round about.

Psalm 124 lauds the Lord's sovereignty over everything in heaven and on earth. This is the quality of saving power that easily rivaled anything man could do or that all the opponents of believers could experience.

Conclusion

Psalm 123 holds up for our meditation the person who has suffered and yet is willing to wait for God's vindication. Martin Luther applied this psalm in this manner:

> This is a deep sigh of a pained heart, which looks round on all sides, seeks friends, protectors, and comforters, but can find none. Therefore, it says, "Where shall I, a poor despised man, find refuge? I am not so strong as to be able to preserve myself; wisdom and plans fail me among the multitude of adversaries who assault me: to Thee I lift mine eyes, O Thou that dwellest in the heavens." He places over against each other the Inhabitant of heaven and the inhabitants of earth, and reminds himself that, though the world be high and powerful, God is higher still. What shouldest *thou* do, then, when the world despises and insults thee? Turn your eyes thither, and see that God, with his beloved angels and his elect, looks down on thee, rejoices in thee, and loves thee.

Of course it is hard to leave injustices, snubs, and wrongfully delivered rebuffs in the hands of God. Our natural impulse is to demand that everything be immediately retracted or *we* will make trouble. But it may well be that our chastening is from the Lord. If redress is needed, even when God uses it for our good, he alone can administer that redress at the proper time. In the meantime, let us stand with our eyes glued on heaven until he gives us the promised relief. Even if all men should wrong us, speak ill of us, and plot against us for our destruction, yet he remains our friend and our refuge. We never to feel forsaken like children who awaken suddenly and find the room empty. His eyes of love are always there if we will only lift up our eyes and look.

Psalm 124 immediately recalls the times when God indeed has delivered us. How frequently have we been in the path of danger and have never even known it, because the angel of the Lord swept our path clean. So why do we doubt the same when we are aware of the danger? God calls us to remember the numerous times we have been aware of his deliverances and to use them as benchmarks for every new hour that we face.

There is the need to praise the Lord who has not given up on us or turned us over to our enemies. The Maker of heaven and earth never wearies. He is never exhausted from extending his helping hand. He will ever save and deliver all who call on him.

As dramatic as the deliverance of Daniel from the lions, so also can the deliverance of all of God's saints be. Let all of us confess, "'If the LORD had not been on our side, ... if the LORD had not been on our side when men attacked us,'" we would have been eaten up, drowned, and washed away. "Praise be to the Lord. ... Our eyes look to the LORD our God till he shows us his mercy."

Questions for Thought and Discussion

1. What is the relationship between our submitting to the Lord and his extending mercy or graciousness to us in our time of need?

2. How much contempt, ridicule, and unfair accusation must a believer bear before taking personal steps to vindicate and clear his or her name? Does it make any difference if the accusers are believers or not?

3. Can we always claim that God is only on our side and not on the side of our enemies? In times of war, believers on both sides of the conflict conscientiously believe that they are in the right. Is this correct?

4. If the snare needs to be broken at times, does this imply that God often waits while we are suffering only to deliver us just in the nick of time? Does God necessarily need to deliver every time, regardless of any other concerns? Do we need to fear that God will forego deliverance under certain conditions?

5. What connection do you see between God as being the Maker of heaven and earth and the fact that our help is in his name?

Psalm 123   Pleading with Submission

Isaac Watts   (C. M.)

O Thou whose grace and justice reign
   Enthroned above the skies,
To Thee our hearts would tell their pain,
   To Thee we lift our eyes.

As servants watch their master's hand,
   And fear the angry stroke;
Or maids before their mistress stand,
   And wait a peaceful look;

So for our sins we justly feel
   Thy discipline, O God;
Yet wait the gracious moment still,
   Till Thou remove Thy rod.

Those that in wealth and pleasure live
   Our daily groans deride,
And Thy delays of mercy give
   Fresh courage to their pride.

Our foes insult us, but our hope
   In Thy compassion lies;
This thought shall bear our spirits up,
   That God will not despise.

Psalm 124   Blessed Be the Lord

Isaac Watts   (C. M.)

Had not the Lord, may Israel say,
Had not the Lord maintained our side,
When men, to make our lives a prey,
Rose like the swelling of the tide.

The swelling tide had stopped our breath,
So fiercely did the waters roll,
We had been swallowed deep in death;
Proud waters had o'erwhelmed our soul.

We leap for joy, we shout and sing,
Who just escaped the fatal stroke;
So flies the bird with cheerful wing,
When once the fowler's snare is broke.

For ever blessed be the Lord,
Who broke the fowler's cursed snare,
Who saved us from the murd'ring sword,
And made our lives and souls His care.

Our help is in Jehovah's Name,
Who formed the earth, and built the skies;
He that upholds that wondrous frame
Guards His own saints with watchful eyes.

❖ **5** ❖

When Your World Is up for Grabs

Insecurity during the Journey

The latest quest of modernity is the search for fail-proof security systems. Nowadays, it is not uncommon to see almost everything bolted down and attached to some type of alarm. There are security systems available for homes, cars, boats, library books, clothing stores, and even credit cards.

Although the forms and modes of living have changed beyond belief since the times of the Old Testament saints, the cries of the insecure, the undefended, and the disinherited have not changed. Regardless of how secure many of us may feel, there come to all of us times when we are suddenly left with a real or imagined sense of insecurity. When the strong suddenly become weak, when the trusted suddenly become untrustworthy, when the healthy suddenly become ill in either body or mind, the issue of security looms high on our lists of priorities.

Psalm 125 takes us to the heart of our fears about possible losses, disappointments, bereavements, clouded minds, broken hearts, or bodily harm. It is a joy to know that even under the strain of such forebodings, our trust in the Savior can grow and become like a mountain.

Our Confidence in the Security of the Righteous (Ps. 125:1–3)

The anchor for all fainting and fearful hearts is put forth in verse 1: "Those who trust in the LORD" are secure. The Lord is our anchor. Here is a new look at the reality lying behind surface perceptions. We are transported into the invisible reality that is the most certain and stable of all reference points. The mighty presence and power of the living God ought to capture our thinking and be more real to us than anything that may threaten us.

The stability of the believer is likened to Mount Zion itself. Just as Mount Zion is unmovable, so is the believer who trusts in the Lord. Instead of letting circumstances drive us, our fixed point of reference is to be found by attaching our hearts to the Lord himself. Those who choose to do so cannot be moved because their hearts are established and set.

Certainly Christians experience their share of troubles. Ask believing parents who have just lost a baby in a tragic crib death. Christians are not always insulated and spared from facing such problems and pressures. Often, instead, when we cannot understand, and the tears and the hurts mount so that we feel we could burst, we are given a place of refuge. We will not be left shaken and seismically stirred into emotional turmoil that knows no respite or comfort. Believers who depend solely on the Lord will endure forever. They are God's unshakeables.

But there is more. Believers are surrounded. Once again the analogy comes from the mountains, only this time it is not Mount Zion. Verse 2 compares the mountains that surround Jerusalem and the Lord who mightily surrounds his people. Even as Elisha's servant had to have his eyes opened in order to see the hills filled with an enormous army of angels that exceeded in number the forces of the Syrian army that encompassed Samaria (2 Kings 6:17), so too do we need to have our eyes opened in order to see God's provision for us.

If only we were more sensitive to the invisible forces that God has provided for our security, we would not fret as much. As Elisha reminded his doubting servant, "Those who are with us are more than those who are with them" (2 Kings 6:16). The fact that we don't always see these forces does not diminish the reality of their presence or the fact that God will be a wall around us just as the mountains are a wall around Jerusalem.

The threats to modern-day life are awesome indeed. Too many of us have been reduced to frightened worrywarts. We worry about the loss of a job, the loss of health, or the loss of reputation. But there are larger fears that hover over us, such as the threat of a cremating nuclear blast, or political or economic takeover by forces that oppose freedom and democracy, and the fear of natural disasters such as floods and fires, or violence against people and property. But the greatest fear that anyone in this world should have is the fear of facing the coming Lord Jesus without ever having made peace with him. This should be the world's greatest source of insecurity and fear. However, there is no excuse. The man who visited our planet two thousand years ago promised to come back to rectify all injustice, evil, and unbelief.

Consequently, the pilgrim of this psalm could say with confidence what appears to be the theme of this chapter:

> The scepter of the wicked will not remain
> over the land allotted to the righteous,

> for then the righteous might use
> their hands to do evil.

The extended length of the lines in verse 3 may be the psalmist's way of indicating that we have reached the heart of his message to all the insecure.

The authority (as signified by the scepter) and power of the wicked nations will not come to rest on the soil of Israel's inheritance. More frequently than Israel would like to admit, one foreign ruler after another had marched into the land. But verse 3 notes that in no way will this subjugation to foreign invaders ever be a settled or permanent arrangement. Foreign rule will not "remain." Oppressors will never finally take over the land originally promised to the righteous because if God allowed evil to remain unrequited in the land forever, it would affect the behavior of the righteous. They too would be tempted to engage in murder, robbery, dishonesty, partiality in the law courts, and like practices of the wicked.

As a further indication of God's security system, the backs of the wicked will be broken and those who trust in the Lord will be rooted and established in the Lord. They will not be moved by anything negative, and they will know that they are surrounded by the living God. The scepter of wickedness will not come to rest on the inheritance of those who trust in the Lord. No matter how great the forces of evil may grow, the wicked will never be a match for God. Pharaoh tried and failed. Sennacherib tried and had to go home empty-handed and with 185,000 fewer troops. All this after he had boasted that he would shut up Hezekiah like a bird in a cage.

Our pilgrim can be confident. The unseen reality of God's security transcends all that appears to be at hand and threatening. God is on the throne. Therefore, no matter what may happen to us we can be secure.

Our Prayer for God's Reward and Retribution (Ps. 125:4–5)

The promises of God were not meant to eliminate the need for prayer. Rather, they were intended to teach us what we ought to pray for. Thus the promise of verses 1–3 are now followed by prayer.

The "upright in heart" are the focus of the pilgrim's prayer for God's work. "Upright" comes from the Hebrew stem word that means that which is straight or direct. These individuals are straight shooters. They have given their hearts unreservedly to the Lord. There is no duplicity or double-dealing in them. Their greatest joy is to put their trust in the Lord.

Their petition is for God to do good to those whose hearts are perfect toward him. God is the great equalizer in life. He alone is the one who is in charge of doing good. All good comes from him. Therefore, our prayers ought to be addressed to him rather than to the modern idolatries of our day.

On the other side of the ledger, the pilgrim prays that those who have specialized in crookedness might be trapped by the logic of their own wickedness. If the wicked have chosen the road of crookedness, let the Lord reveal to them the consequences of their choices. Otherwise let them reap what they have sown.

The sides are delineated—wickedness and righteousness. The Lord will banish all who deviate from the path of purity and truth. They too will end up in the place where all evildoers go.

The psalm closes with a prayer for peace on Israel. Of course, almost everyone talks about peace, but the only true peace anyone will ever know is the peace that comes from God. That is why we must appeal to God for the peace of Israel. This is not spiritual Israel: there are no clues that we are to take it that way. Rather, God will conclude history by doing exactly what he said he would do for Abraham, Isaac, Jacob, and David. When he restores peace to Israel, then he will also have completed the great work of providing redemption for all who have called on him from every tribe, tongue, and nation.

Such a teaching leads the pilgrim naturally into the thought that God has done great things for all of us. This is the theme of Psalm 126.

Our Joy Over God's Great Works (Ps. 126:1–3)

Did you ever have something happen to you that was so wonderful it seemed as if you were dreaming? Something similar to that is depicted here in this psalm, which almost certainly reflects Judah's return from the Babylonian captivity.

Verse 1 begins, "When the Lord turned our turnings" (literal translation), that is, when he restored or brought us back from our captivity in Babylon. Judah had been allowed to return home under the beneficent hand of the Medo-Persian king Cyrus because God had touched his heart. Cyrus established a policy of repatriation and contributed to the rebuilding of the captured country's temple, which had been destroyed during the conquest.

To be standing again in the ancient ruined streets of Jerusalem seemed like a dream come true! The returned exiles were filled with dreamlike wonderment and astonishment. Their mouths filled with songs of joy (v. 2) and laughter. Nehemiah, in referring to this same return from captivity, explained, "the joy of the Lord is our strength" (8:10). Here is a joy that truly fills the whole being. It lifts the countenance. It possesses the soul. Most other joys are fleeting and hollow by comparison.

From the perspective of the other nations it will be clear that "the Lord has done great things for them" (Ps. 126:2). This theme probably first appeared in Joel, a book that many date in the ninth century B.C. There Joel also states that the Lord has done great things (2:20–21). We can join in the theology of this passage by singing:

> Great things he has done,
> Great things he has done,
> Great things he has done,
> He has done great things for us.

Indeed, the people in Joel's day dreamed as did the people in the day of the psalmist. But all of this is only preliminary to a future day of the Lord. What the biblical dreamers experienced in being released from captivity is only a preliminary stage to that final day when God will do more than just release captives from conquering nations.

At this same time in the postexilic period, God sent another prophet, Haggai, to Israel. He warns the people not to despise the day of small things (Hag. 2:3–9), because the final day when Christ will intervene into the ordinary affairs of men and nations is directly linked with every work that the Lord has done in the historic process. We must not isolate the previous deliverances of our Lord from that final grand deliverance. Restoration of all believers is directly linked with the final restoration of Jews to their homeland. God will restore Israel to its homeland not to show that he is partial to them or that they are his pets; he will do it to complete and fulfill the promise that he made to Abraham, Isaac, and Jacob.

So many of the phrases of Psalm 126 reproduce verbatim the expressions and Hebrew text of Joel that it is hard not to see some type of association between them. For example, "then it was said among the nations" (v. 2; cf. Joel 2:17, 19) and "the LORD has done great things" (v. 2; cf. Joel 2:21) are more than coincidence. If mere coincidence is ruled out, then we may note the future context of Joel 2, as a time not only when God pours out his Spirit on all mankind, but also as a time when he will finally act in gathering up Israel from among the nations and will establish his kingdom forever. No wonder the returned exiles were like those who were dreaming!

Our Prayer for God's Great Work
(Ps. 126:4–6)

The first blush of joy, which the exiles experienced on returning, was immediately dimmed by the realities of life. After all, only a small remnant had returned. The land had lain fallow for seventy years. It had been neglected for too long and was choked in a tangle of weeds. Other nationalities had moved in. Wild animals had taken over and posed a new threat. Jerusalem's walls and the temple still lay in a heap of ashes and the immediate attempt to rebuild had been met with rebuff, criticism, and discouragement.

Thus, like our own pilgrimage in spiritual things, the exciting and dramatic activities often lead to the stubborn realities of life. The prospects were dark and there were too few workers for the enormity of the task that lay before the returned exiles. Therefore, verse 4 repeats the first line of this psalm, "Turn, O Lord, our turnings," or to put it more idiomatically, "Restore our fortunes."

The work of restoration was not completed during that postexilic return. The people looked forward to the last day as well as to the immediate future. They prayed that God would act in their immediate future, but they knew any action God might take at that time would only be an earnest payment, a down payment, and would be a mere taste of what the climactic act and work of God will be like when he brings history to a close.

Two metaphors in verses 5 and 6 carry the thought of the end of history forward: streams in the Negev (the desert to the south of Judah), and the harvest a farmer reaps. Accordingly, when God completes the restoration, it will be as sudden and as overwhelming as the raging torrents pouring down the dry wadis and gulches of the Negev. When that happens, what has been a dry, desolate wasteland will suddenly be transformed into a flower garden. When I was in Israel in 1980, I witnessed how the spring rains transformed what had been mere sand to a massive garden of grass and flowers. God will flood the land with men and women once again!

In farming, all the joys of harvest are hard won and long awaited. There are at least three laws of harvest noted in Psalm 126. First is the law of sowing. In spite of many sorrowful disappointments and threatening clouds, the farmer must patiently work on and continue sowing. He knows that the harvest is in the future and that if he is patient it will come at last.

The second law of the harvest is the law of death. Before anything can sprout, the seed must die in the ground. One wonders how often our Lord reflected on this truth as he made the twenty or so annual trips up to Jerusalem before he faced the cross. Jesus had taught in John 12:24, "I tell you the truth, unless a kernel of wheat falls to the ground and dies, it remains only a single seed. But if it dies, it produces many seeds." Where there is no dying of seed, there is no reproduction—in the spiritual world or in the natural world of plants!

The third law is the law of multiplication. The harvest always exceeds the quantity of the seed sown. A little bag of seed will yield many sheaves of grain. Nothing is more typical, even to this day, and nothing is more delightful than to see a farmer returning to his Israeli village in the evening with his donkey laden down with sheaves of grain. He "will return with songs of joy carrying his sheaves with him" (v. 6).

The grandest harvest of all is coming at the end of the age. As Amos 9:13–14 instructs us,

> "The days are coming," declares the LORD,
> "when the reaper will be overtaken by the plowman
>   and the planter by the one treading grapes.

New wine will drip from the mountains
and flow from all the hills.
I will bring back my exiled people Israel;
they will rebuild the ruined cities and live in them.
They will plant vineyards and drink their wine;
they will make gardens and eat their fruit.
I will plant Israel in their own land,
never again to be uprooted
from the land I have given them."

And what is true of God's final wrap-up of history is also true of the spiritual realm. Many have gone forth in service for Christ sowing with tears as they have tried to see men and women, boys and girls come to know Christ. But if they are willing to follow all three laws of the harvest, they too shall reap even though they have gone out often weeping in the hard work of winning and discipling individuals for the Savior.

Conclusion

Haggai notes how the early years of the return produced only drought conditions in the land. They sowed, but they brought in little. They ate, but they were never satisfied. They drank, but their thirst was not quenched—all because they did not see the connection between the production of the land and the progress they had made in spiritual obedience.

However, when these returned exiles repented and turned to the Lord in obedience, the Lord began to prosper the work of their hands. Does this tell us something about the general direction of the economy of a nation and the trust that, at least, a remnant exhibited before the Lord?

Could it be that the kingdom of God languishes around the world while many in the professing body of believers go about tending to their own interests? Do we still place our homes and jobs ahead of the house of God and the call to minister and to serve in Christ's name?

We need a special moving of the Spirit of God in our midst to convict us of this serious breach of commitment, if we have neglected God's work. We must go forth once again sowing the seed of the Word of God with joy and tears. Our Lord will give the increase, but we must pray, "O Lord, restore our fortunes once again even as you did it for Israel long ago and as you will do it once again as you bring history to its grand finale."

Questions for Thought and Discussion

1. Are we capable of shoring up our insecurities with a solid confidence in the living God or are we just putting up a brave front? Is the phrase "God helps those who help themselves" a truth we should take seriously?
2. How can God do good to us when Scripture tells us that there are none that do good; not even one? On what basis is it possible for God to promise to act beneficently to anyone if our sinfulness is so pervasive?
3. Can the promise that God will banish all those who persist in perpetuating crooked ways be equated with the annihilation of the wicked? If so, why are so many Scriptures so insistent that the duration of the punishment of the wicked is just as long as the extent of the eternal life enjoyed by all believers?
4. Note the three tenses of joy in Psalm 126 with verse 3 in the present tense being the pivot verse and concept for the whole psalm. How are past joys a barometer for present joy in Christ and how does that affect the future joy?
5. How can sowing in tears be connected with reaping in joy?

Psalm 125   The Soul That Leans on God

Isaac Watts   (C.M.)

Unshaken as the sacred hill,
And firm as mountains be,
Firm as a rock the soul shall rest
That leans, O Lord, on Thee.

Not walls nor hills could guard so well
Old Salem's happy ground,
As those eternal arms of love
That every saint surround.

While tyrants are a smarting scourge
To drive them near to God,
Divine compassion does allay
The fury of the rod.

Deal gently, Lord, with souls of Thine,
And lead them safely on
To the bright gates of Paradise,
Where Christ their Lord is gone.

But if we trace those crooked ways
That the old serpent drew,
The wrath that drove him first to hell
Shall smite his follow'rs too.

Psalm 126   A Spiritual Harvest Assured

Isaac Watts   (C.M.)

When God revealed His gracious Name,
And changed my mournful state,
My rapture seemed a pleasing dream,
The grace appeared so great.

The world beheld the glorious change,
And did Thy hand confess;

My tongue broke out in unknown strains,
    And sang surprising grace:

Great is the work, my neighbors cried,
    And owned the power divine;
Great is the work, my heart replied,
    And be the glory Thine.

The Lord can clear the darkest skies,
    Can give us day for night,
Make drops of sacred sorrow rise
    To rivers of delight.

Let those that sow in sadness wait,
    Till the fair harvest come,
They shall confess their sheaves are great,
    And shout the blessings home.

❖ 6 ❖

When You Face Domestic Pressures

Families during the Journey

Christmas Day 1989 brought unexpected relief for the citizens of Romania who over the previous forty years had experienced enormous deprivation and brutality. The government and the family of Nicolae and Elena Ceausescu, which had held a stranglehold on all finances, food, and power in Romania, was toppled.

In the wake of their subsequent execution, it was disclosed that the Ceausescus had spent eight hundred million dollars on a 150-room villa in the center of Bucharest. This unfinished, so-called House of the Republic in the heart of the capitol occupied 49,500 square yards of land in the center of three square miles. Approximately fifteen thousand workers had labored for years, often rebuilding some parts until they suited the fancies of the Ceausescus. (The marble foyer was rebuilt eight times!) This house was their all; from the gold fixtures in the bathrooms, to the gold tureens, finger bowls, and picture frames. The House of the Republic was not intended to be a place in which to receive guests. It was the Ceausescus' private hideaway—even though in 1989 it was still four years from completion.

If only the Ceausescus had believed what Solomon teaches us in Psalm 127: "Unless the LORD builds the house, its builders labor in vain" (v. 1). And that is exactly what happened, for they were never able to enjoy one moment of what they had so systematically stolen over a twenty-four-year period from the starved population.

Solomon composed this psalm as he was enlightened by the Holy Spirit and as he exercised his administrative duties and mingled with the people. He learned not only from his own experience but also from the people's lot how vain and unproductive were worries over providing for one's welfare in daily life.

The Vanity of Household Management Without God (Ps. 127:1–2)

Everything in life, not just the building of houses or palaces, depends on God's blessing and protection. When God withholds his blessing, it matters not how swiftly one runs the race or how strong one is in battle (Eccl. 9:11).

In order to appreciate fully the depth of this psalm, we must first realize that "builds the house" (v. 1) does not simply refer to the material construction of buildings. It refers to everything that goes on in connection with life in the home. The Germans call it *haushallten*, "managing the household," while Aristotle (*Politics* 1.3–13) entitled it *oeconomia*, from which we get our word *economics*. A household economy includes primary relationships such as those of master to servant, husband to wife, and father to children as well as secondary relationships such as gaining property and getting wealth. Psalm 127:1 shares a similar expression with Exodus 1:21, where God gave the two midwives families (literally "built [them] into houses"). Solomon's purpose is not to take us into house architecture or construction methods. Rather, his purpose is to describe a believer's marriage and to show how believers ought to conduct themselves as fellow heirs of the grace of life and as managers of households.

Normally one would assume that domestic life would depend on how hard one worked. The American dream is that one can be anything he or she wishes to be. All one has to do is throw oneself into the task, which amounts to motivation. But to this line of thinking, Solomon, who of all persons ought to know, says no!

Who, then, is this who so affects household management and marriage? It is he of whom Solomon declares, "Unless the LORD builds the house, its builders labor in vain." Mere human activity is to no avail if God is left out.

Three times "in vain" occurs in verses 1–2. The vanity of human activity is set forth in five futile pursuits: labor at building a house, guarding a city, rising up early to work, staying up late to work, and eating the food earned by heavy labor. As long as God is not in these activities, they are a vain exercise. Solomon, the consummate statesman and master builder, realized that without God all is vanity. For thirteen years Solomon built his own house, and for seven years he built God's house. He had fortified cities and had built city gates over which archaeologists still marvel. But Solomon acknowledged utter dependence on the Lord. Only God can prosper the works of our hands, no matter how diligent or industrious we may think we are or how deserving we believe ourselves to be.

The lesson Solomon learned and pointed out to us is still the same: We must depend on God's graciousness for all the blessings we covet most—happiness for our families, success for our labors, security for our country, as well as the advancement, productivity, and wealth of our times.

Luther commented on this text:

> This passage alone should be enough to attract people to marriage, comfort all who are now married, and sap the strength of covetousness. Young people are scared away from marriage when they see how strangely it turns out. They say "It takes a lot to make a home"; or "You learn a lot by living with a woman." This is because they fail to see who does this, and why He does it; and since human ingenuity and strength know no recourse and can provide no help, they hesitate to marry. As a result they fall into unchastity if they do not marry and into covetousness and worry if they do. But here is the needed consultation: Let the Lord build the house and keep it, and do not encroach upon his work; the concern for these matters is his, not yours.... Does it take a lot to make a house? so what! God is greater than any house. He who fills heaven and earth will surely also be able to supply a house, especially since he takes the responsibility upon himself and causes it to be sung to his praise. [*Luther's Works*, 45:324]

What a pity that for over a thousand years the church fathers and other principal churchmen of the day allegorized Psalms 127 and 128. Even great people of the past such as Chrysostom and Augustine depicted domestic life as being secular and common, a veritable hindrance to all spiritual life. In their view, if one were to strive for spiritual perfection, one had to abstain from marriage, devote oneself to celibacy, and retire from this world. Thus, the very joys and relations that this psalm commends and recommends were denied and overlooked through a process of isolation from the realm over which God had declared himself to be the Builder. It was assumed that the two psalms could not mean what they appeared to mean; therefore they became allegories of divine relations and joys. The "wife" who was like a fruitful vine became the church, the spouse of Christ; the "shoots" were the sons and daughters of God. But Luther became the first teacher to successfully revolt against this tyranny of the church fathers and the Scholastic writers of the Middle Ages. He reinstated the family to its full dignity and beauty as put forth by God in these two psalms. Luther's interpretation of Psalms 127 and 128 was a protest against the dominant theology of celibacy as being God's preferred way to holiness. Thus began one of the greatest social revolutions that Europe had ever known up to that time.

The text does not say, "The Lord builds the house, so there is no need for anyone to work." It is work, not needless worry or covetousness, that is approved. The type of work that is "in vain" is the type for which one can imply or boast, "I did it myself."

Solomon has much to say in the Book of Proverbs about the legitimacy of work. The lazy were to be punished if they would not work. Proverbs 10:4 teaches, "Lazy hands make a man poor, but diligent hands bring wealth." Nevertheless, "The blessing of the LORD brings wealth, and he adds no trouble to it" (Prov. 10:22). Even the ant provides a good model for humans to follow because "it stores its provisions in the summer" (Prov. 6:6–8). But poverty will come on those who insist on "a little sleep, a little slumber, a little folding of the hands . . ." (Prov. 6:10–11; cf. 24:30–34). Again, "diligent hands will rule, but laziness ends in slave labor" (Prov. 12:24). Or "a sluggard does not plow in season, so at harvest time he looks but finds nothing" (Prov. 20:4).

Since God usually gives us nothing unless we work for it, it is possible for us to become confused and think that we are actually the ones providing for ourselves. However, God's allowing us to work is only another evidence of his goodness to us. Should we think differently, remember what Luther asks: Who put the silver and gold in the mountains? Who fertilized the soil of the field that is ripe with harvests of grain, grapes, and all sorts of produce? Who gave animals and birds the ability to reproduce, thereby providing food for men and women? God preceded us and laid out the blessing that people would later discover.

Thus the greatest problem of the human condition is solved with a simple conditional statement: "Unless the LORD builds the house, its builders labor in vain." All other economic theories that delete this fundamental proposition are at once rejected by this universal principle in Psalm 127:1. Let us earn our livelihood in a diligent and honorable way, but let us entrust the building and the worrying to the Lord.

What has been said of all domestic relationships ("building the house") is now said of the city and the nation. "Unless the LORD watches over the city, the watchmen stand guard in vain" (Ps. 127:1). If proof of this text is needed, simply ask any of the standing armies, secret police, or militia of the recently liberated countries in Eastern Europe. Ceausescu felt that no one could ever penetrate his secretariat, but his watchmen guarded it in vain when God said it was over.

Let the people found a city and establish a nation. Let the nation become a world leader and have wealth and economic power. Nevertheless, unless that nation lives under the guidance of God, the question must be asked: "Will that nation's prosperity endure? Will that nation continue for long?" Unfortunately, nations blindly conclude that longevity is all a matter of cleverness, clout, and courage. Meanwhile, God watches and waits patiently for the moment to "foil the plans of the nations, [to] ... thwart the purposes of the people" (Ps. 33:10), for "The LORD knows the thoughts of man: he knows that they are futile" (Ps. 94:11). Indeed, "He breaks the spirit of rulers; he is feared by the kings of the earth" (Ps. 76:12). Even pagan King Nebuchadnezzar concluded after his sanity had been restored to him, "No one can hold back his hand or say to him: 'What have you done?'" (Dan. 4:35).

Solomon instructed all kings, princes, senators, judges, and mayors to be watchful and diligent in the performance of their duties, but he also instructed that they must not think that that was all there was to the matter. They were made to realize that ultimately only the Lord can watch over a city. No one must arrogantly presume that his or her own effort would be that which secured the land and guaranteed its prosperity: it is the Lord who watches over the city or all is in vain.

If circumstances go well, then we, in our godless condition, become arrogant. This God will not tolerate. If circumstances begin to turn sour and fail, then we, in our faithless pride, begin to worry, lose heart, and doubt God. Neither arrogance nor worry is justified before God. The believer is never to be afraid, for "the LORD is my light and my salvation—whom shall I fear?" (Ps. 27:1).

In our frantic efforts to make a living (or a fortune), we make a wreck of our lives. In our desperate national effort to be militarily prepared for every eventuality, we have drained our resources and developed a national neurosis, not to mention such a huge debt that no one knows how we shall ever be able to repay it. How did we ever forget the condition of this text: "Unless the LORD builds ... unless the LORD watches"?

I do not argue for lack of preparedness, nor for laziness. Rather, we must be ever aware that God is in control. Humans may propose, but it is God who disposes. Solomon teaches in Ecclesiastes: "The race is not to the swift or the battle to the strong, nor does food come to the wise or wealth to the brilliant or favor to the learned" (9:11). It is God who is the giver of all that befalls the whole human race.

Some feel that if they could get up earlier and go to bed later, they would be able to unlock treasures in all areas of human endeavor. But this striving too is futile if God is not in it and if it does not please God to give the increase. Then even when for a moment success appears to have been achieved, it nevertheless often slips through the fingers and disappears.

Working hard for a living without realizing that ultimately it is God who gives me the strength to work and the goods I use in my labor will only produce "the bread of sorrow." A refusal to believe that it is God who nourishes us will only make our work more difficult, grievous, and unpleasant. But for those who conclude that all things, including the management of one's household and the guarding of the nation, are from God; they are the ones he loves and the ones to whom he grants sleep. No matter how strenuous the work or how demanding the issues that must be faced in a day, the believers who trust God will live carefree, uncluttered lives. They will sleep as if they hadn't a care in the world: "Cast your cares on the LORD and he will sustain you; he will never let the righteous fall" (Ps. 55:22; cf. 1 Pet. 5:7).

The Vanity of Marriage and Raising Children Without God (Ps. 127:3–5)

Suddenly, the psalmist seems to have lost his train of thought or it appears that another psalm has been incorrectly attached to verses 1–2 of Psalm 127. What could be the connection between verses 1–2 and 3–5?

The transitional thought is to be found in the points already made in verses 1–2. The connection is a comparison between the arrogant, anxious, and distrustful person who gets up early and works late (but all for nothing), and the humble, calm, trustful person who is so at rest with his Lord and his world that he can sleep whether things are good or bad. Consequently, "a heritage" and "a reward" await this person (vv. 3–5).

It is not just my livelihood, my housing, my job, my breath, and my nation's security that are gifts from the Lord; even my children are not the result of my own powers. The conception of a single child is wholly the work of God. Why then are we so bent on securing goods and possessions when it is up to God whether we possess anything or not?

In fact, Solomon compares children with "arrows in the hands of a warrior" (v. 3). Therefore, just as a warrior shoots his arrows wherever and whenever he chooses, so God deals with us! It is equally amazing to watch how husbands and wives or nations achieve extraordinary stature in life for which they have never really striven. For God's "beloved," circumstances have a way of turning out much differently than one would have thought.

Likewise, we are just as dependent on God as we are on children, who are the life of a home and a nation. Children, like the arrows in a quiver, are a means of protection. Thus when we are surrounded by our sons, we are safe and we are assured of their assistance. Children are God's gifts—God's heritage, or reward.

It is interesting to note that verse 4 mentions (literally) "children of youth," meaning those who have not yet become householders or guardians of the city. It is such dependent ones as these that God still guides or shoots as his arrows while they are still in their homes and in their own cities. God will do with them as he wills, but we must also be faithful to do our part in raising these tender arrows. God is concerned about more than theology, the supernatural, grown adults, or nations; he is vitally concerned over the baby in the crib and the adolescent in those difficult years of maturation. God's heritage and reward to mankind are these "children of youth" (v. 4), whom he holds in his hand as an archer would hold his arrows—secure and ready for aiming.

The blessedness of a full quiver is also asserted in this text. God's desire is that we recognize children not as being necessary nuisances, but as being gifts from God. The recognition that children are gifts is not a mundane or secular approach to spiritual things; it is the Bible's embracing of all things as coming under the sovereign control of God.

Because God wishes us to have our quivers "full of children," he must assert the following principles:

1. Don't be stingy about the number of children we wish to have. We may only be cheating ourselves and the Lord who wishes to give us an inheritance.
2. Don't put off having children until our assets are more stable and we have the money to give them all the finer things in life. Children were meant to increase our effectiveness, not diminish it. Furthermore, have we forgotten already that "unless the LORD builds ...," we can provide nothing for our children, no matter how prepared we may think that we are.
3. Children are the best retirement program going, for they are living assets. No one will put us to shame in the city gate when we have many children to come to our defense. Children are God's inheritance and his reward.

No weapons or armaments are mentioned in verse 5 as being necessary for defense against enemies. Children will merely speak the word and stand up for their parents, even though such blessing may not be without some persecution and trouble. Wherever people are prospering under the good hand of God, one may also expect that the evil one will not be far behind in attempting to stir up trouble. Ungodliness cannot stand righteousness, either in households or in cities. But God has provided his special source of defense in the heritage of the sons of our youth.

Happiness for each household, then, lies in its resting in the Lord, for unless he builds the house, we will all work and strive to no avail.

Happiness for each nation, city, or principality likewise rests in our trust in the Lord. Indeed, over the lintels of all the homes of the city should be these Latin words: *Nisi Dominus frustra*, "Except the LORD builds, we labor in vain."

Questions for Thought and Discussion

1. Why did it take the church so many years to discover the "secular" meaning of Psalm 127? Could there be other texts that even among today's enlightened Bible believers are still being resisted?
2. Name as many areas as you can to which the concept of "managing a household" or the Lord's building "economic" relationships applies.
3. How vulnerable is the city or country that you presently live in, assuming the truth that only the Lord is able to watch over a city? To what degree is the future of a nation conditioned on that nation's believing and acting on this truth?
4. Are children really "a pain in the neck" or is there a real blessing in having sons and daughters? How many is a quiver full? Is it a sin to deliberately enter marriage with the idea of avoiding raising any children?
5. How are children a permanent inheritance from the Lord? Will they come to our defense when we need them?

Psalm 127   Contentment

Isaac Watts   (C.M.)

If God succeed, not all the cost
And pains to build the house are lost;
If God the city will not keep,
The watchful guards as well may sleep.

What if you rise before the sun,
And work and toil when day is done,
Careful and sparing eat your bread
To shun that poverty you dread;

'Tis all in vain, till God hath blest;
He can make rich, yet give us rest:

Children and friends are blessings too,
If God our sovereign make them so.

Happy the man to whom He sends
Obedient children, faithful friends:
How sweet our daily comforts prove
When they are seasoned with His love!

❖ 7 ❖

When Your Mate and Children Delight You

Marriage during the Journey

It was Martin Luther who pointed out the differences between Psalm 127 and 128. Psalm 127 treats both national and domestic life; Psalm 128 lays greater emphasis on the home, matrimony, and the family. He rightly saw the home and marriage as being the fountainhead of what good civil government hoped to be. As Luther explained it, "For of houses or families are made cities, of cities provinces, of provinces kingdoms. Household government, then, is with reason called the fountain of policy and political government, for if you destroy the one, the other cannot exist." Luther concluded, "Wherefore to this Psalm we give this title, that it is an Epithalamium or Marriage Song, wherein the Prophet comforteth them that are married, wishing unto them and promising them from God all manner of blessings."

So opposed was Luther to the medieval glorification of celibacy that he never tired of praising matrimony as being a divine institution. No wonder he loved Psalms 127 and 128 and quoted them so frequently! He also composed both a German and a Latin paraphrase of Psalm 128. This paraphrase may well have been inspired by a sermon Luther preached on January 17, 1524, on the wedding at Cana (John 2:1–11). The German title was *Wol dem der im Gottes furcht steht.* The translation is that of MacDonald and the tune usually suggested (though four different melodies are found in hymnals of the sixteenth century) is "Tune of St. John Huss," or the melody of "Jesus Christ, Our God and Savior." Here is Luther's hymn, "Happy Who in God's Fear Doth Stay":

> Happy who in God's fear doth stay,
> And in it goeth on his way;
> Thine own hand shall thee find thy food,
> So liv'st thou right, and all is good.

> So shall thy wife be in thy house
> Like vine with clusters plenteous,
> Thy children sit thy table round
> Like olive plants all fresh and sound.

> See, such rich blessing hangs him on
> Who in God's fear doth live a man:
> From him the [old] curse away is worn,
> With which the sons of men are born.

> From Zion God will prosper thee;
> Thou shalt behold continually
> Jerusalem's now happy case,
> To God so pleasing in her grace.

> He will thy days make long for thee,
> With goodness ever nigh thee be,
> That thou with thy sons' sons may'st dwell,
> And there be peace in Israel.   (L.M.)

This psalm teaches us that there are three elements in a happy and honorable domestic life:

the element of industry (vv. 1–2)
the element of tranquility (vv. 3–4)
the element of godliness (vv. 5–6)

The Element of Industry (Ps. 128:1–2)

Psalm 127 concludes in verse 5 that the individual who had his quiver full of children is blessed. Psalm 128 picks up on this same theme, blessedness, but here it is the person who fears the Lord and who walks in his ways who is blessed.

All too often we become proud of our prosperity, letting it go to our heads. However, if we were to regularly acknowledge that everything we have is from God, we would not be able to boast in our prosperity. What do we have that we have not first received from our Lord as a gift? Therefore true blessing and happiness can come only from above.

Those who have faith in the living God will not fail even when called to go through trouble enough to have frightened the heartiest of believers. In Hebrews 11 we are told that by faith they endured cruel mockings, beatings, scourgings, bonds, imprisonments, and stonings. They were sawn asunder or slain with the sword. They wandered about in sheepskins, being destitute, afflicted, and tormented; yet, they all received a good report! Their lives exhibited faith in operation.

Psalm 128 opens with a pronouncement of happiness on all who fear God and who walk in his ways. The fear of the Lord does not mean we fear him or cower in a corner at the sound of his approach. The fear of God is, instead, an attitude of trust in and commitment to the God who loves us, and is expressed in our desire to live by his Word.

For those who experience this God-sent happiness, life takes on a whole new tone and zest. The result is a commitment to working to glorify God. Whereas others who do not fear God sow seed and labor with their hands and minds, their labor does not bear fruit; they sow in vain and their enemies get to eat whatever little is raised (Lev. 26:16). This scenario is repeated so frequently in Scripture that it could easily be a major theme. The price for failing to trust and fear God is like running against the grain of the universe. Disobedience results in numerous negative consequences that affect the whole of one's life. In Deuteronomy 28:30–33 we are warned, with Israel, that we may be pledged to marry a woman, but as a consequence of our disobedience another will take her; we may build a house, but another will live in it; we may plant a vineyard, but another will enjoy its grapes; our possessions will be confiscated before our own eyes— including our own sons and daughters (see also Amos 5:11 and Micah 6:15 for a very similar type of situation).

Even more frightening should be the prospect raised in Ecclesiastes 6:1–2: God allows us to pile up possessions, wealth, and honor, so that we lack virtually nothing our hearts could desire; however, God does not give to us the ability to enjoy these things. Enjoyment of possessions remains separate from the possessions themselves so that we might be driven back to God and to a condition where we might love, trust, and fear him.

Those who fear God will be productive. They will benefit from what they produce. Eating the "fruit of [our] labor" or the "labor of [our] hands" is a picturesque phrase regarding our reaping the proper reward for all our industry and efforts. It is a picture of a quiet, peaceful country life with no fear that the harvest will be trampled underfoot by invaders. Neither will the tasks that are performed be invalidated by some misfortune that repeatedly wipes out everything in spite of our best efforts. There is no cause for anxiety for the future.

The psalmist teaches elsewhere, "Show me your ways, O LORD, teach me your paths" (Ps. 25:4); and "those who turn to cooked ways the LORD will banish with the evildoers" (Ps. 125:5). Therein lies the believer's approach to the ordinary world. A person can set out for work fearing and loving the Lord or refusing to do so, but the results of all his or her work and industry can be tabulated in advance.

The Element of Tranquility (Ps. 128:3–4)

In verses 3 and 4, the psalmist subtly makes us feel the calm and deep peace that pervade the godly household. There follows a picture of comeliness and cheerfulness that usually only mothers and wives can add to a home. The pilgrim's wife is likened to a "fruitful vine" (v. 3), a symbol that is not restricted to fertility, but one that also speaks of grace and delicateness. Clearly, the psalmist regards monogamy as the biblical ideal. Only one vine is spoken of here.

This concept of a fruitful vine must not be distorted and abused. No encouragement should be given to the misconception that the wife is merely a receptacle whose usefulness is restricted to reproduction only. How base and uninformed can we get? She too is "an heir with [her husband] of the gracious gift of life" (1 Pet. 3:7). Any demeaning of her is at once a demeaning of her Lord at the same time!

The godly wife is "within [her husband's] house" (v. 3), in contrast to the adulterous and wayward wife whose "feet never stay at home; now in the street, now in the squares, at every corner she lurks" (Prov. 7:11–12). The godly wife finds her delight in her home, her family, and her husband. They rejoice in her and she finds her joy in them.

The olive tree is a symbol of productiveness, freshness, vigor, and health, and this couple's children are like it. They are sturdy, thriving individuals who contribute to their environs.

Meal times were likely a special delight; filled with laughter and excited news from the other members of the family. In our day family members are so busy that we can barely find at least one meal each day in which all the members of the family are present to enjoy each other and to experience what it means to be in community. Families were meant to help us with the process of socialization and to nurture awareness of one another's needs and joys. But selfishness and the demands of time have worked against this happy picture of family tranquility and happiness.

Such tranquility does not naturally come from the mere fact that we are in a family; it must spring from our personal faith in the Lord. The theme of verse 1 ("blessed are all who fear the LORD, who walk in his ways") must not be overlooked in our attempt to describe that tranquility here. Our faith is not faith in labor. Neither is it faith in success, or faith in unusually favorable conditions in life or of faith in relationships that will unlock doors for us; it is exclusively a faith in God alone.

Verse 4 repeats the theme of verse 1 by reminding us that "thus is the man blessed who fears the LORD." We have here a God-fearing father, a comely, gracious wife, and a family of sturdy, vigorous, healthy children. That is the scene of a quiet, tranquil, and happy life. But let us not forget that this setting is incomplete without any evidence of faith in the Lord or obedience to his Word that that faith prompts.

The Element of Godliness (Ps. 128:5–6)

The source of blessing is from Zion, the abode of God. Psalm 134:3 expresses the same thought: "May the LORD, the Maker of heaven and earth, bless you from Zion." Once more in these Psalms of Ascent we are reminded of the Aaronic benediction of Numbers 6:24, "May the LORD bless you."

All gifts in life are from the One who made heaven and earth. When he smiles on us, we are enriched and enlarged in one benefit after another. But when, because of our sin, he turns his back to us, we are left in the dark and are bereft of both the ordinary and special gifts of life.

The psalmist prays: "May the LORD bless you from Zion all the days of your life" (v. 5). All other things being equal, long life seems to be a sign of God's approval and/or his mercy. Verse 6 expresses the same sentiment in terms of "see[ing one's] children's children." This is a pleasant prospect for all parents. Of course, the experience may not be pleasant in an evil world where many things that have nothing to do with the nature of the individual often intrude. Thus, just as an apple tree will be faithful to its own nature in growing tall, spreading its branches, sprouting blossoms, and producing apples, only to have an unexpected frost, a tornado, or a hurricane destroy it all, so some are cut down early in life through no fault of their own; the fault lies in an evil world where sin still abounds. Consequently we must be careful not to judge prematurely merely by appearances.

The appeal to a long life as an all-encompassing motive for fearing the Lord is found at least six other times in Proverbs:

> The fear of the LORD adds length to life,
>   but the years of the wicked will be short. [10:27]

> The fear of the LORD is a fountain of life,
>   turning a man from the snares of death. [14:27]

> Humility and the fear of the LORD
>   bring wealth and honor and life. [22:4]

These so-called worldly emphases in the Proverbs have their roots in the doctrine of creation and in the law of God. From these passages it is easy to deduce that the fifth commandment is not the only passage that promises "long life" in exchange for honoring one's parents (Exod. 20:12). The same promise was repeated after the Red Sea crossing: "If you listen carefully ... and keep all [my] decrees, I will not bring on you any of the diseases I brought on the Egyptians" (Exod. 15:26). It was also repeated in Moses' last words: "Take to heart all the words I have solemnly declared to you this day ..., they are not just idle words for you—they are your life" (Deut. 32:46–47).

Taken out of context these promises sound like works-righteousness, but in their rightful context of creation and the overall law of God they simply affirm and celebrate the special place that redeemed creatures, made in the image of God, have in God's world. There is a union of the good with life itself. This does not mean that every ethical person will always be rewarded with material and financial prosperity. This is no health, wealth, and prosperity message. But in God's plan for our spiritual good there is also a plan for our human wholeness. The Bible does not segregate the profane or material world from the sacred world as we in the West do. Biblical Christians saw no conflict between faith and practice, belief and action. Hence long life was part and parcel of the same world as was fearing God.

The psalm ends with, "Peace be upon Israel" (v. 6). This is exactly how Psalm 125, another of the pilgrim psalms, ends.

Conclusion

The New Testament teaches that godliness with contentment is great gain (1 Tim. 6:6). Therefore, let us live quiet, peaceable, and godly lives to the glory of God. Life's effectiveness must not always be measured by the amount of fuss and fury that goes on around us. Works are not always to be the measure of what is or is not being accomplished.

Instead, let us come back to the basics of fearing God, walking in his ways, and enjoying for a while the results of our labors. Let us take joy in our spouses, our children, and the times we can share with them.

Only then will we see the prosperity of the Lord. Only then will blessing flow out from the presence of God.

Questions for Thought and Discussion

1. Using a concordance, do a word study on "the fear of the Lord." What elements would you say should go into the definition of this great theological phrase?
2. How do you picture the ideal wife or the ideal husband? How do you agree, and how do you disagree, with contemporary expectations and redefinitions of what a husband or a wife should or should not be?
3. What role do children play in a Christian view of the family? Is it still possible in our modern world to have such a view?
4. How is the prosperity of Israel and Zion linked to the believers' present happiness, if at all?
5. Define a "happy" person according to this psalm. Now contrast that picture with the contemporary view of happiness and success.

Psalm 128   Family Blessings

(C. M.)

O happy man whose soul is filled
With zeal and rev'rend awe!
His lips to God their honors yield,
His life adorns the law.

A careful providence shall stand
And ever guard thy head,
Shall on the labors of thy hand
Its kindly blessings shed.

Thy wife shall be a fruitful vine;
　　Thy children round thy board,
Each like a plant to honor shine,
　　And learn to fear the Lord.

The Lord shall thy best hopes fulfill
　　For months and years to come;
The Lord, who dwells on Zion's hill,
　　Shall send thee blessings home.

This is the man whose happy eyes
　　Shall see his house increase,
Shall see the blessed saints arise,
　　And leave the world in peace.

When Opposition Mounts

Enemies during the Journey

Psalm 129 closely resembles Psalm 124 in subject, style, and structure. Both psalms are constructed on the same model. The theme of both is deliverance from one's enemies, though the theme is sufficiently varied so that the two psalms complement one another. The opening verses of each psalm are based on the same pattern. Each gives a backward glance to the captivity in Egypt, and each uses two metaphors. Psalm 124 speaks of a swollen mountain torrent and a bird escaping from a broken snare; Psalm 129 speaks of a plowman drawing long furrows and of the grass on the rooftops that springs up, but withers.

The central affirmation of the psalm is found in verse 4: "But the LORD is righteous; he has cut me free from the cords of the wicked." Here we have the great principle on which Israel's assurance of final deliverance rests: the righteousness of the Lord. And that is the same assurance that all believers worldwide can have. Because our God is just and altogether "in the right" (literal translation), all who have ever experienced suffering, conflict, or oppression can rely on God's righteousness to loose all the bonds of the oppressors.

The setting of this psalm is definitely from the countryside. Because I was born and raised on a farm I find myself drawn to this psalm. I can still hear Dad instructing me, as verse 3 reminds us, that it is a matter of rural pride that all the furrows opened by the plow be perfectly straight. "Pick out an object at the other end of the field," Dad would say, "so that you may drive straight toward it and make that first furrow as straight as an arrow."

Then there are the scenes of the grass sprouting on the roofs in the early spring only to wither in the hot sun of summer. One can almost hear the reapers calling their greetings out to those passing by the fields being harvested: "The blessing of the LORD be upon you." The scene is altogether reminiscent of one of those in the Book of Ruth (2:4). The pilgrims, in turn, called back to the reapers, "We bless you in the name of the LORD."

Before we look at the psalm, let us look at the verse that Isaac Watts based on this psalm. He set the psalm in what is known as common meter. A sample of well-known hymns written in common meter are Watts's "O God Our Help in Ages Past," "Joy to the World," and "Am I a Soldier of the Cross," as well as others such as "All Hail the Power of Jesus' Name," "O for a Thousand Tongues to Sing," and "Amazing Grace." When one remembers that these psalms were meant to be sung and used in both private and corporate worship of God, it is more than appropriate that we also should understand them and use them in a modern musical and devotional form.

Up from my youth, may Israel say,
Have I been nursed in tears;

My griefs were constant as the day,
   And tedious as the years.

Up from my youth I bore the rage
   Of all the sons of strife;
Oft they assailed my riper age,
   But not destroyed my life.

Their cruel plough had torn my flesh
   With furrows long and deep,
Hourly they vex my wounds afresh,
   Nor let my sorrows sleep.

The righteous Lord when on His throne,
   Looked with impartial eye
Measured the mischiefs they had done,
   Then let His arrows fly.

How was their insolence surprised
   To hear His thunders roll!
And all the foes of Zion seized
   With horror to the soul.

Thus shall the men that hate the saints
   Be blasted from the sky;
Their glory fades, their courage faints,
   And all their projects die.

What tho' they flourish tall and fair,
   They have no root beneath;
Their growth shall perish in despair,
   And lie despised in death.

So corn [grain] that on the house-top stands
   No hope of harvest gives;
The reaper ne'er shall fill his hands,
   Nor binder fold the sheaves.

It springs and withers on the place:
   No traveller bestows

A word of blessing on the grass,
Nor minds it as he goes. (C.M.)

Now let us look at the psalm itself. Often life seems to become one long and wearisome battle. This is how Israel felt: "From my youth up, I have been a person of strife." From the time that Israel was in Egypt, it was as if life had been just one battle after another. First it was Egypt, then the desert clans. Canaan gave no respite, nor had the Syrians, Assyrians, or Babylonians been any kinder. Life was "the pits" for Israel, or so she thought. However, in spite of the heavy opposition, the enemies, one after another, never gained a final victory over the nation, anymore than do the enemies of today's believer.

At this point the imagination of the poet is stirred and he likens the activity of the tormentors to a man plowing an arable field. However, here the picture is not of a tillable field. Instead, the psalmist depicts the enemy making long, deep furrows down the back of the people of Israel. One can visualize the plowman throwing his full weight from handle to handle of the plow as the oxen pull it along. There could not be a more graphic picture of the sufferings and miseries of the nation. How steadily the oxen trample the backs of the people. What deep incisions the plow opened in the shoulder blades and down the spinal column.

Suddenly a deliverer springs to Israel's defense: "But the LORD is righteous" (v. 4). The Lord God is the great emancipator. No enemy or foe can prevail against those who belong to the Lord. He it is who will cut us free from the cords of the wicked. The allusion here must be to the traces that harness the oxen to the plow. The Lord slashes the traces and the oxen are free from the drudgery of pulling the plow through the hard soil. Similarly, the Lord himself releases Israel from her cords of bondage and delivers her.

If this psalm reflects the postexilic era in Israel, then not only had Israel felt the plow of the conquering Babylonians, but they had felt the same biting pain of adversaries such as Sanballat the Horonite, Tobiah the Ammonite, and Geshem the Arabian—not to mention the Samaritan looters who insolently ran over the territory as if they owned everything.

The second strophe, verses 5 to 8, divides the psalm into two equal parts. Once again the imagination of the psalmist uses a metaphor, but this time he points not to a figure of oppression or conquest. Instead he selects an image that is so ordinary, fleeting, and valueless that it is sure to provoke a memorable impression for a good while to come.

What could be more common than grass that grows on the flat rooftops in Israel? If one were really observant, one could spot grass growing on the roofs during the rainy season. In the cracks and crevices of these roofs of mortar, ashes, and sand one would find that some grass seeds or grains of barley or wheat had lodged in the crevices only to germinate as soon as the rains came. Then, because there was no depth to the soil, this grass could never amount to anything.

So it was to happen to all of Israel's enemies—and so it will happen to all of our enemies as well. They will wither and dry up. They will be as harmless as dried grass, as worthless and as useless as grass that never had a chance to do more than sprout.

Verse 7 tells us that no reaper is even interested in this grass. It lives and dies for no obvious purpose. The reaper cannot fill his hands with it, nor can the gatherer put in his sickle to cut down the wheat or fill his or her hands with it. And there is no reason to do so, for it never matured into anything useful—not even grass. It had withered all too soon. No one would pass by the roofs and say as was the custom to those who reaped in the fields: "The blessing of the LORD be upon you." Nor would there be the usual response shouted back, "We bless you in the name of the LORD" (v. 8).

The contrast in scenes is startling indeed. What do the few straggly strands of grass facing certain extinction have in common with scenes of harvesting? Nothing. Likewise, the wicked who have tried to inflict their evil on the sons of God are in reality more like the withered grass on the housetops than like the bountiful harvest that men joyfully reaped with delightful greetings to all who passed by.

The singing of this psalm did more than strike a patriotic note. It called all of God's people to recall that their true defense and strength was none other than the righteous Lord. He alone was able to deliver them from adversaries. Only God could plant the seeds of destruction in those who opposed the people of God. God was to be trusted. He is more than just, fair, and righteous in all his ways. He is good to those who trust him, but not necessarily to those who do not. Therefore it would be well for us not to be overly hasty and worked up about the apparent success of the wicked or the way they seem to prosper.

To be sure, the wicked often plow long, deep furrows into the backs of the righteous. But God will notice the backs of the elect and will suddenly cut the traces of the plowman's animals. Thus, in the end the righteous will sing over their harvest while the wicked will wither like the grass on the rooftops.

Final and complete victory is assured to the believer. We must rest our case with the same Lord who delivered Israel in the past. Two assurances are given in this psalm, each matching the two equal strophes:

> our God has overcome our enemies (vv. 1–4)
> our God has shamed and turned back our enemies (vv. 5–8)

Conclusion

We may have been greatly oppressed from our youth, but in no way can our enemies ever say that they have gained the victory over us. Our God is righteous; he has freed us from the cords of the wicked. Thanks be to his marvelous name. No matter how stormy life may seem to be in the midst of strife, the believer can always count on the fact that the deliverer, our Lord, is never far away from any one of us. Cutting remarks will be healed with the soothing balm of Gilead. Our God will cut the traces that harnessed us like oxen to the plow and will set us free. The psalm offers hope to all who trust in the Lord.

Questions for Thought and Discussion

1. If Israel felt that she had been oppressed from her youth, does this tell us something about the necessity of persevering in prayer?
2. How is it possible to be oppressed without being defeated? The psalmist seems to say that the enemies never had the satisfaction of totally conquering Israel.
3. Define what it means when we say that the Lord is righteous, just, and always "in the right." Give several examples.
4. Is it really true that the wicked flourish only for a brief season and then they wither and disappear from the scene? How does one know this is true? Give examples.
5. In what way do oral blessings, given to one another, communicate an actual benefit or advantage? (Even our blessing of someone who sneezes? Is this also biblical?)
6. Does the exchange of greetings/blessings between the travelers and the reapers suggest the content of our speech to one another in everyday life? Do our curses in moments of wrath and despair actually handicap the lives of our children, friends, or enemies? Will God honor these words?

When Guilt Overwhelms You

Forgiveness during the Journey

[Psalm 130] is a tiny gospel announcing the truths which men of every age need to know; it is a tiny manual, recording, in brief musical phrases, the large simple experiences which are common to all good men. [Samuel Cox, *Pilgrim Psalms*, 218]

Psalm 130 has also been called *De profundis*, for it begins with that magnificently moving phrase, "Out of the depths I cry to you, O LORD." It is the sixth of the famous seven Penitential Psalms found in the Psalter, namely, Psalms 6, 32, 38, 51, 102, 130, and 143. This psalm is a plea to God that he forgive. From his own experience of having been forgiven, the psalmist exhorts those in similar need of God's gracious forgiveness to wait and look for mercy, for it will surely arrive.

The story is told of Martin Luther, who in 1530 was in the fortress of Coburg. On four separate occasions during one night he experienced what seemed to be three blazing torches come in his window. Troubled in mind and spirit, he fainted, and when he revived, he suffered from a severe headache. His servant quickly poured oil of almonds into his ear and rubbed his feet with hot napkins. Luther begged his servant to read a portion from the Book of Galatians, during which he fell asleep. When Luther awoke, happy with relief and rested from his sleep, he enthusiastically invited, "Come! To spite the devil, let us sing the psalm *De profundis*, in four parts."

The structure of the psalm is simple and plain. It has four strophes or poetic paragraphs, each exhibiting a pair of divine names. Each strophe is made up of two verses. The psalm has two allusions to the same metaphor—a shipwrecked sailor crying to God "out of the depths" (v. 1). From the blackness of the night he desperately yearns for, watches for, and hopes for the break of day (v. 6).

Unlike the authors of Psalms 124 and 129, who also used graphic pictures to convey their messages, the author of Psalm 130 does not give us any details of the image. There are no references to broken wreckage bobbing precariously on a roaring surf. Nor is there a reference to a wretched sailor clinging to a few pieces of timber torn apart from the ill-fated vessel, a sailor longing for the first rays of dawn.

Psalm 130 does not have a reference like that of the escaping bird (124:7), the swollen mountain stream (124:4), the plowman digging long furrows down the back of his adversary (129:3), the quick-growing and easily withered grass on the rooftops (129:6), or the reapers greeting those passing by the harvest field (129:7–8). The charm of Psalm 130 is to be found in its simplicity. Except for one repetition in verse 6, there is no other elaboration.

Its most pronounced literary feature is that it introduces the divine name Adonai three times (cf. Psalm 86 where Adonai occurs seven times). This is the name for God that stresses the fact that he is actively ruling the world and intervening in it by judging, guiding, blessing, and punishing where needed. The name *Adonai* (translated "Lord," lower-case letters), alternates with Yahweh (translated "LORD," uppercase letters). In verses 1–2 there is the cry for help that goes up to Yahweh (= "the God who will be [there]"); the LORD who sits high above all the storms of time. Then in parallelism with that name of Yahweh (= LORD), verse 2 says, "O Adonai ["Lord"], hear my voice." Again, in the next strophe of verses 3–4, it is affirmed that if Yah (a shortened form of Yahweh [= LORD]), the eternal God dwelling in the heavens, should keep a record of iniquities, O Adonai, the near Lord of men, who could ever hope to survive such scrutiny? Finally, in the third strophe reliance is affirmed in Yahweh, who sits high and lifted up in his temple, and in Adonai, who is asked to intervene on behalf of humanity.

Here, then, is a song of forgiveness. It was one of Luther's favorites, as well as the favorite of millions of other believers. Someone asked Luther what his favorite psalms were. He replied, "The Pauline Psalms." When pressed to define which these were, he responded, "The 32nd, the 51st, the 130th, and the 143rd. For they teach us that the forgiveness of sins is vouchsafed to them that believe without the law and without works; therefore are they Pauline Psalms; and when David sings, 'With Thee is forgiveness, that Thou mayest be feared,' so Paul likewise says, 'God has concluded all under sin, that he may have mercy on all.' Therefore none can boast of his own righteousness, but the words, 'That Thou mayest be feared,' thrust away all self-merit, teach us to take off our hat before God and confess *gratia est non meritum, remissio non satisfactio*—it is all forgiveness, and no merit" (as cited by F. Delitzsch, *Biblical Commentary on the Old Testament* [Grand Rapids: Eerdmans, 1949], 13: 302).

When sinners sense the awful weight and the burden of their own sin and despair, how does one get relief? This psalm not only tells us how to spell r-e-l-i-e-f, but it supplies us with the *steps* for obtaining it.

Our Cry for Help (Ps. 130:1-2)

In the psalms it is not unusual for troubles to be likened to flood waters (cf. Pss. 18:16; 42:7; 69:1, 2, 15; 88:6, 7; 124:4). These need not be interpreted as being the waters of chaos, implying proximity to Sheol and final separation from the Lord. They most likely refer to the depths of the raging sea in this psalm. In his moment of grave danger, the psalmist cried out to Jehovah/Yahweh (= LORD). The verb is not present tense marking a long experience of beseeching up to the present moment. It conveys that there was a decisive moment that he clearly remembers in the past.

The psalmist is doing some real soul searching. There is no attempt to bribe God or to make himself look good in the eyes of God. There are no vows taken such as, "I'll never touch another drop of that stuff again," or "I promise I'll change and never do anything like that again." The psalmist makes no specific request. He is greatly humiliated by his own sin and like a child who has just been rebuked or punished, he wishes only to be restored to favor and to be absolved of any harm caused. God cannot be coerced or bribed into extending forgiveness; it is always a matter of his gift and free grace.

The practice of the synagogue priest was to read the lessons from the Law and the Prophets and to address the congregation from a platform. But prayers were offered from a lower position near the ark of the covenant, where the scrolls of the Scriptures were kept, a practice that is said to trace itself to the opening words of this psalm. Hence the Talmud will always say, "He went down to the ark," or "He went down to read the prayer."

Our psalm begins by turning from Yahweh on high to Adonai, the Lord who is immanent, active, and close to all who call on him. The plea is that God will hear, or be attentive to the voice of my supplications, or my cry for mercy. It may be worth noting that the word used for "hear" or "be attentive" occurs only here and in 2 Chronicles 6:40 and 7:15—

Solomon's great dedicatory prayer for the temple and the call for revival found in 2 Chronicles 7:14.

Our Assurance of Forgiveness (Ps. 130:3–4)

Unfortunately for the sinner, we are often most reluctant to come to God and to ask for his forgiveness, for we know how frequently we have disappointed him in the past. But God is willing to deal with us better than we deserve.

On the one hand, God has "set our iniquities before [himself]" (Ps. 90:8). Job knew this as well: "If I sinned, you would be watching me" (10:14). On the other hand, fortunately for all of us, the Lord has not punished us according to what we deserve. Had he chosen to do so, no one would be left standing in his sight.

The best news of all is that "with [the LORD] there is forgiveness." Literally, it is *the* forgiveness. God has not proceeded according to stringent legal standards. Not only would one be left without defense, but there would be no forgiveness. Verse 4 is directly connected with verse 3 in the Hebrew text by "for" (Hebrew, *ki*).

The word *forgiveness* is uniquely used in the Old Testament. Its only subject is God. As a noun (though the verb occurs frequently), it is found only here, in Daniel 9:9, and in Nehemiah 9:17 (the adjective appears only in Psalm 85:6). The Lord is willing to forgive in order that his name alone may be feared—so that only his name may be glorified. He is the sole author of our salvation. All our attempts to glory in our works or our own goodness are put to shame, for his mercy is exalted instead of his justice.

God is not a Scrooge-like bookkeeper who rewards each according to what they deserve and no more. He mercifully pardons without any meritorious prompting. As the prophet reminds us in Isaiah 55:6–9, our Lord doesn't think the way we think, neither does he act the way we act, for his thoughts and his ways are higher and different than our thoughts and ways: He will abundantly and "super-freely" pardon. God will grant the forgiveness that we need. He forgives not so we might think lightly of our sin, but that we might magnify his compassion and his grace.

The clause *therefore you are feared* sounds like a strange outcome of forgiveness. But forgiveness should lead to true worship and true reverence and knowledge of God. Forgiveness should not lead to licentiousness. It is not a license to sin. It should lead to the fear of the true worship of God. It is an obedience that is motivated by love for the Lord who has forgiven us so much.

Our Confidence in the Lord (Ps. 130:5–6)

Oftentimes our despair is caused by the fact that we have performed so badly; we have hurt so many that there is no possibility of making up for all the mess and for rebuilding the future. But God's forgiveness changes all of that. Through forgiveness we do have a future and there is reason to have confidence in tomorrow.

The Hebrew text of verse 5 says, "My soul is unto [or belongs to] the Lord." The psalmist throughout the long weary night has not contemplated the wretchedness of his sin in vain. He (and we) put confidence and hope in the Word of God—and here that word is the word of forgiveness.

As the watchman waits anxiously for the dawn, we too wait for the Lord. This longing for the break of dawn was graphically illustrated in the autobiography of Harold E. Hughes, the former governor of Iowa. Hughes served with General George Patton in the invasion of Italy in World War II. He recounts a hair-raising experience he once had while waiting for dawn to arrive. Said he,

> My outpost was far forward where I'd watch for four hours.
> I started up the steep mountain path in pitch darkness, feeling
> the thin communications wire for guidance. As I crept along

my heart leaped at every falling pebble. I neared the outpost and whispered the first half of the password, "Trafalgar," and waited the answer "square." Not a sound. I called out again: "Trafalgar." Deadly quiet. My insides congealed and I lay there, fingers gripping the dirt. Finally, I inched forward to the hole and reached in, expecting to find a body. I dropped into the pit, picked up the telephone, which worked, and settled down with my rifle and waited. The hours crawled by as I waited. Would the sun never rise? "Let me live through this night," I continued to plead until daylight when I was relieved [of my duty]. [Harold E. Hughes, *The Man from Ida Grove: A Senator's Personal Story* (Waco: Word, 1979), 59]

Few examples, such as this one of waiting for the dawn after a horrible night of frightening terror, can better express the longing of the soul for the dawning of God's loving mercy upon our gloomy spirits.

Our Redemption from Sin (Ps. 130:7–8)

Now the long wait is over—at least for those who cry out of the depths of their despair and the agony of their sin to the living Lord. Redemption from sin rests not in our works, but simply and solely in God's "unfailing love" (v. 7). The word *hesed* is one of the most beautiful words found in the Old Testament. It occurs 250 times and few if any English words can accurately mine the riches found in this word. It can be translated "grace," "mercy," "lovingkindness," "loyal love," "unfailing love." But every one of these concepts stress that everything depends on the unmerited favor of God which he freely and graciously gives to all who from the depths (*de profundis*) will cry to him for forgiveness from sin.

The extent of God's free gift is made clear in verse 7. The gift is more than a mere promise. He has paid in full for our release. There is full redemption in him. He will pay all that we owe. The amount he pays is enough to dismiss forever all charges against us. Over against the weakness of our faith and the slimness of our hopes, the redemption of our Lord exceeds everything we could have hoped for or imagined.

For all those who have protested, "But my sins are too horrible; I've failed too many times and I have committed the most heinous sins known to mankind," our Lord responds most deftly, "With me there is abundant redemption." God will redeem, not only Israel, but all who call on him, from "all their sin" (v. 8). That excludes no one.

God's forgiveness is not just from the punishment due because of our sins; it also includes breaking the power of those sins. We can be set free from sin's bondage. This promise comforts us with the fact that complete and final redemption (in the New Testament manner) is here offered on the basis of the forgiveness that one day will be paid for at Calvary, but is now freely offered by our loving Lord.

Conclusion

In today's culture it is all too popular to regard the root problem of the human race as being the loss of self-esteem rather than the Bible's depiction of the matter as being the result of sin. Our ultimate need is salvation from sin and the hope of forgiveness. It just is not true, as one popular television pastor has averred: "Reformation theology failed to make clear that the core of sin is a lack of self-esteem" (Robert H. Schuller, *Self-Esteem: The New Reformation* [Waco: Word, 1982], 98). Salvation according to this scheme is merely to be lifted from shame to self-esteem, self-respect, self-worth, and a new sense of dignity. These may be some of the resulting benefits, but this is not what we need redemption for; our situation is much deeper and more precarious. Loss of self-esteem is only one of the by-products of our sin. Our disease is sin!

It is the memory of our failures before God and the reality of objective guilt that has produced what is so painful and has led to such despair. How sweet is the sound of the declaration, "You are completely forgiven!" It is better than a jury's verdict of "not guilty."

Therefore, we leave all our sin at the feet of the one who alone can give us full and abundant redemption—so free, so gracious, so complete. It is marvelous!

Questions for Thought and Discussion

1. Can you recall an incident (from your own life or some-one else's life) when you were in deep trouble until finally deciding to call out to God?
2. What are some of the reasons people give as to why they are reluctant to ask God for his forgiveness?
3. Because it appears that all one has to do is say, "I forgive you," does that make God's forgiveness cheap? And is forgiveness, whether human or divine, possible with-out someone paying for it?
4. What does it mean to fear God? In what sense is this a natural outcome of our having received salvation?
5. Explain some of the practical ways in which we can wait on the Lord. How does his Word figure into that process?
6. If the salvation that our Lord offers is abundant and full, why do so many attempt to add to it, insisting on signs, gifts, or additional works of grace?

Psalm 130   Pardoning Grace

Isaac Watts   (C. M.)

Out of the deeps of long distress,
    The borders of despair,
I sent my cries to seek Thy grace,
    My groans to move Thine ear.

Great God, should Thy severer eye,
    and Thine impartial hand,
Mark and revenge iniquity,
    No mortal flesh could stand.

But there are pardons with my God
    For crimes of high degree;
Thy Son has bought them with His blood
    To draw us near to Thee.

I wait for Thy salvation, Lord,
    With strong desires I wait;
My soul, invited by Thy Word,
    Stands watching at Thy gate.

Just as the guards that keep the night
    Long for the morning skies,
Watch the first beams of breaking light,
    And meet them with their eyes;

So waits my soul to see Thy face,
    And more intent than they,
Meets the fresh op'nings of Thy grace,
    And finds a brighter day.

Then in the Lord let Israel trust,
    Let Israel seek His face;
The Lord is good as well as just,
    And plenteous in His grace.

There's full redemption at His throne
    For sinners long enslaved;
The great Redeemer is His Son,
    And Israel shall be saved.

❖ **10** ❖

When Your Pride Interferes

Humility during the Journey

Some years ago a woman of mature years with rather dubious vocal gifts experienced a short-lived stardom on the basis of her song, "Will Success Spoil Mrs. Miller?" Whether success spoiled her or not, I do not recall. But the question she posed is more than trivial.

In fact, the same question must still be faced by modern evangelicalism. It is time all believers asked, "Has success spoiled us too?" Given the fact that in the 1976 the cover story of *Newsweek* magazine declared that this was the year of the evangelical, some evangelicals could have said that they had finally arrived. For the first time, many who had never experienced political, economic, and sociological clout were now being sought out and catered to. As a result, pride and haughtiness and a new sense of triumphalism reared its ugly head in our circles.

How appropriate it is that Psalm 131 celebrates the blessed-ness of the person who has a lowly spirit and a sense of modesty and humility about them. And how appropriate it is that this psalm should also be placed just after Psalm 130, which deals with the joy of a person who realizes that his or her transgressions have been forgiven. Forgiveness should humble us. We are undeserving of God's free forgiveness, let alone the fact that our sins have been cleansed and removed from us as far as the east is from the west (Ps. 103:12).

The tone of this psalm reflects the spirit of the one who is called "the sweet singer of Israel"—David. Few can rival the unassuming tenderness of a young David who, after having been announced by the prophet Samuel as king over Judah, steadfastly refused to take matters into his own hands and secure his own recognition as king. Even when it seemed as if providence had delivered King Saul into his hands (lying at David's feet in the dark cave to which David had fled), David still declined to put an end to Saul's life.

Too often, when success, prosperity, and attainments of one sort or another come to us, we become proud, haughty and arrogant toward others and even toward our Lord. David reminds us of this awkward state of affairs in another psalm: "Though the LORD is on high, he looks upon the lowly but the proud he knows from afar" (Ps. 138:6).

Pride has its seat in the individual's heart. When our hearts become exalted and we become too big for our own britches (as the saying goes), we set ourselves up for a fall, individually and as nations, churches, and institutions. For example, the Old Testament relates that "after Uzziah became powerful, his heart was high" (a literal translation). "His pride led to his downfall. He was unfaithful to the LORD his God, and entered the temple of the LORD to burn incense on the altar of incense" (2 Chron. 26:16). In 2 Chronicles 32:25 we read, "But Hezekiah's heart was proud and he did not respond to the kindness shown him; therefore the LORD's wrath was on him and on Judah and Jerusalem." Hezekiah's heart also "was high" (literal translation). Yet another example is Psalm 18:27. David sings, "You save the humble but bring low those whose eyes are haughty." I suppose the reason the psalmist names the eyes as being haughty is because pride betrays itself in the eyes. David makes the same point in Psalm 101:5, "Whoever has haughty eyes and a proud heart . . . him will I not endure."

A frequent partner of pride is ambition. Ambition, of course, can be positive, but all too frequently it exhibits a negative side where the ardent desire for rank, fame, or power may be an inordinate desire. This inordinate desire manifests itself in a person's wanting recognition of accomplishment without possessing the ability to accomplish it. David had learned that he should not scheme, plot, or leap into the fray with an exaggerated sense of ambition. For ten years he fled from King Saul rather than use his obvious military prowess to establish what had been promised to him. For another seven years he ruled in Hebron waiting for God to establish him as king over the whole country. Within those seventeen years he let Shimei curse him, Absalom chase him from his own throne, and Michal, his wife, upbraid him.

David did not pretend to have a false humility. His joy was in contemplating the promises of God rather than in trying to obtain what had been promised to him. And when the spirit of pride arose in his life, as it did when he numbered Israel and then mustered them for war when God had not commanded them to go into war, he returned to God in genuine repentance and unconditional dependence (2 Sam. 24; 2 Chron. 21).

Who can debate the need for the warning that this little psalm gives to us? If ever there was a time in the life of the church, especially in the Western world, when this psalm was needed, it is now.

We Must Not Concern Ourselves with Things Beyond Our Understanding (Ps. 131:1)

One of the dangers in claiming to be humble is that in so claiming our humbleness, we lose it. A favorite story told in religious circles is, "Did you hear about the man who was selected 'The Most Humble Person' at a Sunday school picnic? Well, they awarded him a large button with the inscription 'Most Humble Person' on it. However, they took it away from him at the end of the day because he had worn it!"

Verse 1 of our psalm is no boast; instead it is an appeal to the great searcher of our hearts, the Lord himself. He knows the true state of our innermost being. Not only does the Lord know the state of our hearts, but he alone can give us a quiet and meek spirit. He alone can clear our eyes so that they do not betray our pride. Verse 1 gives us a good working description of pride: a haughty heart, eyes with eyebrows raised in a supercilious arc, and busyness with matters that are beyond one's powers. When these conditions are present, pride can take over one's whole person and rule his or her life. God, however, does not dwell with the proud. If we wish to have the presence of God in our lives, we had better ask for a humble spirit.

But what is this warning about unwarranted concern over matters that are too wonderful or too difficult for us? The word for "wonderful" is the same word that occurs in Genesis 18:14 where the Lord asks Abraham why Sarah laughed when he said that she was going to have a child when she was ninety years old. "Is anything *too hard* (Hebrew *pele'*, or wonderful) for the LORD?" (see also Deut. 17:8; 30:11; Job 42:3; Ps. 139:6).

Some of the things too wonderful, too miraculous, and too difficult for us include:

speculation over mysteries that are beyond our grasp; enterprises that go beyond our strength or abilities.

These may be some of the issues that suddenly begin to sap our energies and strength. They can easily lead to discontent, but Paul teaches us that godliness with contentment is great gain. Why should we seek that which lies outside of our ken? Why should we not be content with the duty that is set before us rather than harboring secret desires for a task that has been assigned to someone else?

We Must Be Weaned from Self-Will and Passionate Cravings (Ps. 131:2)

Two verbs set the pace in verse 2—"stilled" and "weaned." Both depict two graphic pictures of what humility is all about.

To still one's soul is to smooth it down like the ground is smoothed down so that seed will grow (Isa. 28:25). Thus after the farmer has plowed the ground, he sets out to level it with his harrows. Likewise, the plowshare of suffering must be followed with leveling—with the smoothing and soothing of one's own soul, quiet before the living God.

David also likens conquered pride to the weaning of a child from his or her mother's milk. Few illustrations can more graphically express the cost at which our rest has been secured. Anyone who has seen (with animals) or experienced (with children) the weaning process gains an immediate, vivid, picture of the struggle suggested here. Weaning is often the child's (or animal's) first experience of loss. It is life's first lesson in self-denial and self-control. It is one of the first times we realize that we are not always going to get our own way. And what a fuss some of us raise before we learn the lesson! Such fusses are little more than demonstrations of self-will and passionate cravings. But the point of humility is that self must not demand its own way and seek its own desires above everything and everyone else. However, some never learn this lesson and they remain a burden for all whose lives touch their own.

All believers in general and evangelicals in particular must cease their restlessness and selfish fretting. Outbreaks of peevishness are really as juvenile as a bawling baby that refuses to be weaned. We must learn how to quiet our souls and be content with all that God has given to us. Otherwise, pride will remain unconquered.

We Must Place Our Hopes for Success in the Lord (Ps. 131:3)

What David learned as his spiritual secret he now recommends to all in verse 3—"Put your hope in the LORD both now and forevermore."

We must learn how to wait on our God. We in the Western world are too impetuous for our own good. We want everything immediately, if not yesterday. So how can we say that our solid confidence and hope for today and all of the future is indeed in the Lord?—a real part of humility, because we too often want to work out our own salvation. But that will never work in God's kingdom. Putting our hope in ourselves, our times, our jobs, our intelligence, our children, our denominations, and our institutions is both a modern form of idolatry and an obvious sign of a lack of humility.

We are not the masters of our own fate; neither are we the captain of our souls as the blasphemous poem *Invictus* boasts. We are poor beggars with outstretched hands gratefully receiving what we could never have paid for and do not deserve. So where is there any room left for boasting or privilege? There is none. And if that is true for our entrance into salvation, what do we have to offer after we have come

to know the Lord? There is nothing about which we can boast except the one who has done so much for us.

Conclusion

Nothing is more difficult for men and women, who have been called by the grace of God to high and holy service, to realize than the fact that all that we have is lent from our Lord. It is God who has given whatever success and increase we have enjoyed.

If we wish to obtain a picture of a humble evangelicalism, let it be the picture of a weaned child lying peacefully and quietly in its mother's arms. It could hardly be that of an austere, proud, and intolerant Pharisee pulling his robe about himself with an air of aloofness. We must search our hearts to see if we have stolen glory from our Lord over the magnificent buildings we have built. Have we been overly impressed with the burgeoning numbers of students in our schools? Are we proud of the apparent success of the growth of our denomination, of our wealth, of our children's laurels, or of any other matters we believe that we have had a major hand in shaping?

When we busy ourselves over matters that are beyond us, we have overstepped our legitimate boundaries and have entered into the area of pride. But there is a humility that rejoices in what is true, what is good, and what is kind—the cultivation of a quiet and peaceful spirit before God.

By God's grace, we must recover the spirit of that weaned child. We must smooth out the rough plowed landscape of our lives and let the peace of God that passes all understanding flood our hearts and minds to the glory of God.

Questions for Thought and Discussion

1. Is meekness synonymous with weakness? Is a meek person someone who is spineless and without strength

of character? Consider Moses' life and the statement that he was "a very humble [or meek] man, more humble than anyone else on the face of the earth" (Num. 12:31).

2. Is it true that haughtiness and pride locate themselves *primarily* in the heart and eyes rather than in action, as verse 1 seems to indicate? Or is the source of pride to be located elsewhere?

3. How can pride manifest itself in our concern with matters that are too wonderful for us? Is this an invitation to mediocrity or is it a warning against megalomania (an obsession with doing extravagant and grand things)?

4. How important is discipline and gracefully accepting one's losses for becoming a truly humble and quiet person?

5. What role does confidence in and expectation for the future play in shaping the character of the humble and meek spirit before God and other persons?

Psalm 131   Humility and Submission

Isaac Watts   (C.M.)

Is there ambition in my heart?
    Search, gracious God, and see;
Or do I act a haughty part?
    Lord, I appeal to Thee.

I charge my thoughts, be humble still,
    And all my carriage mild,
Content, my Father, with Thy will,
    And quiet as a child.

The patient soul, the lowly mind
    Shall have a large reward:
Let saints in sorrow lie resigned,
    And trust a faithful Lord.

❖ 11 ❖

When You Forget the Past

Remembrance during the Journey

Some days are just more spectacular and significant than others depending on what took place on that date. Psalm 132 recounts one of those days in the life of Israel that was remembered repeatedly as the pilgrims made their way up to Jerusalem for one of the three annual feasts.

King Solomon had assembled anyone considered to be important to prepare for the solemn but magnificent entrance of the ark of the covenant into the newly constructed temple. A large number of people had responded to the royal invitation to be present for this most auspicious event. Crowds thronged Jerusalem streets waiting for the long procession of the elders and priests to pass by with the ark. According to 2 Chronicles 5:3, this event took place during the "festival in the seventh month," which is the Feast of

Tabernacles in the month of Ethnanim (Canaanite name) or Tishri (Hebrew name).

Before dying, David had set apart 4,000 Levites for the purpose of praising the Lord with musical instruments (1 Chron. 23:5). Accordingly, one can only imagine the magnitude of this impressive scene. At the same time that innumerable sheep and cattle were being sacrificed (2 Chron. 5:6), "120 priests sound[ed their] trumpets" (2 Chron. 5:12) and the 4,000 singers joined in one mighty Handel-like hallelujah chorus singing: "He is good; his love endures forever" (2 Chron. 5:13; cf. Pss. 100:5; 106:1; 107:1; 118:1; 136:1).

To the strains of this much-loved chorus in Israel, the line of prestigious Levites moved deliberately, bearing the ark on their shoulders. They entered the Holy of Holies in the sanctuary of God. There, behind the inner veil, beneath the cherubim, they set the ark in its place. As the Levites emerged from the temple, the glory of the Lord, the Shekinah glory, the pillar of fire and cloud, came and filled the whole temple.

As the presence of God filled the temple he thereby indicated his acceptance of their worship. Solomon prayed a sublime prayer that continues to this day to stir our hearts with the beauty, pageantry, and significance of that day. What God thought of all of this is recorded in 2 Chronicles 7:1–2, "When Solomon finished praying, fire came down from heaven and consumed the burnt offerings and the sacrifices, and the glory of the LORD filled the temple. The priests could not enter the temple of the LORD because the glory of the LORD filled it." The people, overcome with the grandeur of the whole scene, and especially with the sudden appearance of fire from heaven, fell prostrate before the living God and picked up the strains of the Levitical chorus still ringing in their ears, "He is good; his love endures forever" (2 Chron. 7:3).

What a day in the annals of human history! Psalm 132 was written to commemorate the completion and dedication of the temple, the highlight of which was the installation of the ark of God, previously separated from its proper place for well over twenty years, into its newly constructed house.

What is more natural than that Solomon should compose a new psalm to celebrate the opening of the temple and the bringing home of the ark of the covenant? And what is more natural than that Solomon should focus on the wonderful promise-plan of God that stretches from one end of biblical history to the other? One sure indication that this scenario is a reliable historical judgment is the fact that verses 8–10 of Psalm 132 are simply repeated, with very little variation, in the 2 Chronicles 6:41–42 description of the conclusion of Solomon's dedicatory prayer for the new temple. It is appropriate that we stress the historical setting and Solomon's authorship of this psalm. This information adds fuller insight as to its meaning and significance.

Psalm 132 falls into two halves, with the second half (vv. 11–18) imitating the first half. The caesura, or break, occurs after verse 10 with the negative verbs *do not reject* and *he will not revoke* (Hebrew *shub* - literally "turn" in both cases) functioning as the hinge or link between the two strophes or halves of the psalm.

Basing Our Petitions to God on God's Past Promises (Ps. 132:1–10)

The first five verses of the psalm are a grateful acknowledgment for the completion of the temple. They are also a statement about the character of Solomon's father, King David, because nothing was as central to David as the building of the temple.

Thus our psalm begins with a request that God "remember David and all the hardships he endured." The request is not that God remember Solomon for all the work he had done, but for all the work David had done. The psalmist is reminding God of David's resolve and determination to build a temple. The idea of constructing a house for God had so engaged David's thoughts that one might justifiably refer to them as being "hardships" or "anxious cares." Even when God refused David the privilege of building this house because his hands were full of the blood of war, he nevertheless had persisted in making every legitimate preparation that he could. Consider the plans he had laid and the materials he had gathered. Consider the plans he had made for the dedication service and for the worship of God. It was this magnanimity, this largeness of heart and mind, this disinterestedness for his own good, this overwhelming generosity, that Solomon now remembered.

Even when God had given David rest from all his enemies (2 Sam. 7:1), he would not rest until the ark of God had also found its resting place (Ps. 132:5, 8). Thus, instead of David's saying that he had done enough for the kingdom and instead of saying that he had suffered enough from King Saul and the Philistines in order to save Judah and Israel, he surrendered his retirement years in exchange for seeing that God's house was begun.

During Saul's reign, the ark of God had been captured by the Philistines. For twenty years it had remained far from the house of God. Getting it back to Jerusalem became one of David's top priorities. He vowed that he would not rest in peace until the ark found its resting place in the Holy of Holies once again. Few, if any, tasks could take precedence. David's vow to God was to "the Mighty One of Jacob" (vv. 2, 5; cf. Gen. 49:24; Isa. 1:24; 49:26; 60:16). Jacob's name is mentioned because he was the first to vow a vow to God when he set up a pillar for a house of God at Bethel (Gen. 28:18–22, hence its appropriateness here).

David calls his cedar palace "the tent of my house" and his bed "the couch of my bed"—good instances of the way in which the patriarchal life fixed itself in the language of the people (J. J. S. Perowne, *Psalms*).

The word *dwelling* in verse 5 is actually "dwellings" (plural) in the Hebrew text. This is likely because it refers to David's purchasing and consecrating of the threshing floor of Araunah where the temple would one day stand (2 Sam. 24), his placing the ark in a fixed abode in Zion, and his providing the materials and plans for the temple. Regarding God's dwelling place we note that Isaiah 66:1–2a teaches that

> "Heaven is my throne,
> and the earth is my footstool.
> Where is the house you will build for me?
> Where will my resting place be?
> Has not my hand made all these things,
> and so they came into being?"
> declares the LORD.

The answer is given in verse 2b,

> "This is the one I esteem:
> he who is humble and contrite in spirit,
> and trembles at my word."

Thus the permanent residence of God rests in the spirit of those whose hearts are broken before him and who, when they hear his word, tremble in repentance of heart, mind, and action.

By now it is clear that Solomon realizes his place in history. As he faces the future, he makes three requests. But before we can consider these three, it is necessary to explain verse 6. Three points in this verse call for explanation: To what does the pronoun *it* refer?; Who or what is Ephrathah?; and What are the fields of Jaar?

It no doubt refers to the ark mentioned in the previous verses or to the rumor about the ark. *Ephrathah* is the ancient name for Bethlehem (Gen. 35:16, 19; 48:7; Ruth 4:11; Mic. 5:2). The *fields of Jaar* are probably a shortened form of Kiriath-Jearim, "the city of the woods," where the ark stayed after it was recaptured from the Philistines and where it remained for twenty years (1 Sam. 7:2). The meaning of verse 6 would then be: "we heard where the ark was, so we said one to another, let us go bring it up into its new abode. Even David in his youth had known of the ark only from hearsay when he lived in Bethlehem as a lad. No one thought much about the ark, for it had all but dropped out of the people's thinking."

The temple was now finished. It was time for change. Solomon's first request was not only that the ark itself be restored to its rightful place but also that God himself would follow it and come into his new dwelling. The words, "Arise, O LORD, and come to your resting place," echo the ancient battle cry that Israel shouted whenever the ark was lifted up and went before them in battle (Num. 10:33–36). But Solomon knew that more than mere outward forms were necessary if the reality of God's indwelling was to be there. If God did not accompany the ark, their moving it was a waste of motion and a sham.

Verse 9 forms Solomon's second request. If we are to experience any type of joy in the service of God, we must act according to things in God's way. Solomon had profited from David's initial mistake of trying to move the ark of the covenant without following the rules as had been specified by God (Exod. 25:15; Num. 4:5–6, 15; 2 Sam. 6:1–23). Instead, David had transported the ark in a cart, much as the Philistines had. They, of course, did not know any better. Hence they were not as responsible as was David. The law was clear: Only the priests could transport the ark.

This meant that only those consecrated and clothed with robes of righteousness could transport the throne of God. Only they could carry it into the center of the worshiping community's life. If we today ignore the need for consecrated servants of God, the lay community will not be properly equipped to worship and serve the living God. We will not be able to sing for joy as did the Israelites.

It is interesting to note that the apostle Paul makes a similar argument in Ephesians 4:7–12. Paul based his argument, by analogy, on Numbers 8 and 18, for there the Levites were "taken" and were "given" to God as gifts in place of the first-born of each Israelite family. Again in Psalm 68:18, citing the Numbers passages already referred to, it is clear that the Lord was able to return to the Father because he had left the Levites to carry out the tasks related to God's ministry. Paul likewise argues that in the same way God has taken some apostles, some prophets, some evangelists, and some pastor-teachers as captives for the equipping of the laity so that the laity might do the work of the ministry. That is why Christ also was able to return to the Father. Thus the connection between Ephesians, Numbers, and Psalm 132.

The climactic request comes in verse 10. It is a request that God not turn away from his servant David. It is a plea that God not reject his plan to bring his anointed through that family. In 2 Chronicles 6:42 the same idea reads:

> O Lord God, do not reject your anointed one.
> Remember the kindnesses promised to David your servant.

David had been promised a kingdom, a throne, and a dynasty (a house) in 2 Samuel 7:16. Moreover, he had also been promised that one of his sons would build a house for God, and that his offspring would be God's son and God would be his father.

Accordingly, when Solomon prayed that God would not reject his anointed one, or the Messiah, he was praying that God would not turn away from him. He wanted and needed the presence of God.

All three of Solomon's requests are based on past revelations and promises of God: a resting place for the ark, the ministry of the priests, and the coming of God's Messiah. Solomon was merely asking God to fulfill what he promised he would do. This is the essence of prayer. The promises of God are not meant to exempt us from prayer, but to show us what it is that we should pray for.

Receiving Our Answers from God's Past Promises (Ps. 132:11-18)

The second half of this psalm mirrors the first half. Here we meet with three answers to the previous three requests. However, we must look at God's vow to David in verses 11-12.

What is the point in forging ahead if there is no reason to have any hope for the future? In David's case there was more than just a mere chance that the future would be bright and certain. God had given an oath that was unconditional and irrevocable. God would never change his mind, his plan, or his intention to benefit the whole world through David's offspring. That is the clear teaching of 2 Samuel 7:13. It is a repetition of the promise that God gave to Abraham in Genesis 15 and 17. In fact, when David finally comprehended what God was promising, he was staggered by both the breadth and depth of that promise. This was nothing less than "a charter for all humanity" (literal translation of 2 Sam. 7:19). God's promise was the whole plan of salvation condensed into a plan that would emerge through this man's family line.

The conditional "if" of verse 12 could not affect the certainty of the promise of God; it could only affect an individual's participation in the benefits of that promise while the promise remained inviolable. God's faithfulness to his covenant would stand in spite of those who steadfastly resisted it—even in the Davidic line itself. Those Davidites had to transmit the blessing even if some did not participate in it.

The first answer from the list of three requests comes in verse 13. A resting place for the ark would be given in Zion, Jerusalem itself. The search for a place had ended. God had always intended to make Zion the place of his abode. It was not a matter of Solomon's choosing Zion—God had already done so. (The original resting place of the ark after the wilderness wanderings had been at Shiloh. Then the ark had been at Bethel for a time [Judg. 20:27], then at Mizpah [Judg. 21:5]; afterward at Kiriath-Jearim [1 Sam. 7:2] for twenty years, and then in the house of Obed-Edom for three months before David finally tried to bring it to Jerusalem.)

The theme of verse 13 is elaborated on in verses 14–15. The connotations we receive from "resting place," "sitting enthroned," and "dwelling" are of permanence. Each of these words has a very rich background and continued use in the Bible. Jesus would not only give to his own rest, but he would be that promised "man of rest." The words *to dwell* imply that the Word, when it became flesh, would come and pup-tent, or tabernacle, in the midst of us (John 1:14). Likewise, Paul teaches in Ephesians 3:17, "May Christ dwell in your hearts through faith, . . . being rooted and established in love." The idea is that this Lord Jesus wants to be Lord and to rule on the throne of our lives. When he comes into the world through the Messiah, or into a believer's heart by faith, he does not come in bits and pieces; he comes to rule, and to reign, and to dwell permanently. He it is who will abundantly bless us and satisfy us with life itself.

Verse 16 echoes verse 9 as it answers the second request. God himself "will clothe his priests with salvation so that her saints will sing for joy." All that God's ministers or full-time servants possess comes from the righteousness that is freely given by God. It is not up to so-called professionals to figure out how to relay joy to God's people. Only Christ can give that joy and put a song on the lips of his people.

Christians are today hesitant to minister for the living God for fear that they will not say or do the right things. But we tend to forget that this is all the work of God. He demands only faithfulness. His messengers are clothed in his righteousness—not their own! Therefore we can relax and not worry. Our portion is his joy. Shout for joy, all you who are his saints.

The answer to the third and final request comes in verses 17–18. It takes up the issue of the Lord's anointed. Solomon speaks of three symbols to describe the Messiah: a horn, a lamp, and a crown. The title *lamp* had already been assigned to David in 1 Kings 11:36, "I will give one tribe to his son so that David may always have a lamp before me in Jerusalem." A horn is often used in Scripture as a symbol of strength and power. The crown on his head gave unmistakable evidence that he was to be God's future ruler. That crown would "shine" or "flourish" and "blossom" even as Aaron's rod did in evidence of his divine appointment.

There can be little doubt that the anointed one is not only God's earthly anointed one from David's house but also God's heavenly anointed one, Jesus Christ. That is God's answer to the inquiry made by David's son Solomon as to whether God would maintain his promise. The answer was that he surely would.

Conclusion

Few things in Scripture or in our lives in general are as central as the promise-plan that God made with Abraham and David. The joyous fact celebrated in this psalm is that God has not, nor will he ever, go back on what he promised.

And central to that promise are the features of a resting place for his presence to dwell, the channel of his blessings through his priests as stand-ins of his righteousness, and the strength, light, and splendor of the rule and reign of the Messiah—first in the hearts of his servants and then over all the world. Hallelujah, what a Savior!

Questions for Thought and Discussion

1. In what ways have you been strengthened and/or encouraged to pray more fervently based on what God has done for you in the past or on the promises in his Word?
2. How central to our thinking and practice should the concept of the resting place of God be for modern believers? Do we miss out on some aspects of theology when we fail to appreciate the significance of "place" in regard to the presence of God?
3. How could God maintain his covenant with David as inviolable and irrevocable while also promising to punish all sin even in the house of David? Did David's offspring have a sure berth in heaven just because of God's unconditional promise?
4. What do you think about the explanation given here for the righteousness of the priests and the doctrine of the ministry as set forth by Paul in Ephesians 4:7–12?
5. Is this psalm a celebration about the certainty that the Messiah will come or is it just about Solomon's appointment to the office of king over Israel?

Psalm 132   God's Habitation

Isaac Watts   (C.M.)

The Lord in Zion placed His Name,
    His ark was settled there;
To Zion the whole nation came
    To worship year by year.

But we have no such lengths to go,
    Nor wander far abroad;

Where'er Thy saints assemble now,
    There is a house for God.

Arise, O King of grace, arise,
    And enter to Thy rest!
Lo! Thy church waits, with longing eyes,
    Thus to be owned and blest.

Enter with all Thy glorious train,
    Thy Spirit and Thy Word;
All that the ark did once contain
    Could no such grace afford.

Here, mighty God, accept our vows,
    Here let Thy praise be spread;
Bless the provisions of Thy house,
    And fill Thy poor with bread.

Here let the Son of David reign,
    Let God's Anointed shine;
Justice and truth His court maintain,
    With love and power divine.

Here let Him hold a lasting throne;
    And as His kingdom grows,
Fresh honors shall adorn His crown,
    And shame confound His foes.

❖ **12** ❖

When Unity Prevails

Harmony during the Journey

The German critic Herder said of the exquisite little Psalm 133 that "it has the fragrance of a lovely rose." And indeed, it does. But even more exquisite is its moving and lovely description of the unity that our Lord wanted to exist among those who belong to him in all cultures, denominations, races, genders, and times.

J. J. Stewart Perowne, one of the abler English commentators on the Psalms, describes the impression that this psalm left on him: "Nowhere has the nature of true unity—that unity which binds men together, not by artificial restraints, but as brethren [and "sistern"] of one heart—been more faithfully described, nowhere has it been so gracefully illustrated, as in this short Ode" (*The Book of Psalms* [London: George Bell and Sons, 1878; reprint ed., Grand Rapids: Zondervan, 1966], 2: 417).

The harmony that God desires for his people is compared to the sacred oil, which flowed from Aaron's beard to the hem of his garment, thereby anointing the whole body for service to God. This concord is also likened to the morning dew, which falls not only on the lofty mountain peaks but also on the lesser hills, again refreshing all and including all within its influence.

Once again the title names David as being the author of this psalm. The exact occasion on which this psalm was composed may be placed in one of two settings, seven years apart. The first may well have been on the occasion of David's coronation at Hebron. After eight years of civil war between the house of Saul and the house of David, "All the tribes of Israel came to David at Hebron and said, 'We are your own flesh and blood. In the past, while Saul was king over us, you were the one who led Israel on their military campaigns. And the Lord said to you, "You will shepherd my people Israel, and you will become their ruler"'" (2 Sam. 5:1–3). Even more vivid is the depiction of this event in the narrative of the chronicler. He painted a most charming picture of that coronation: "All these [having listed the numbers of those who had fought with David] were fighting men who volunteered to serve in the ranks. They came to Hebron fully determined to make David king over Israel. All the rest of the Israelites were also of one mind to make David king. The men spent three days there with David, eating and drinking, for their families had supplied provisions for them. Also, their neighbors from as far away as Issachar, Zebulun and Naphtali came bringing food on donkeys, camels, mules and oxen. There were plentiful supplies of flour, fig cakes, wine, oil, cattle and sheep, for there was joy in Israel" (1 Chron. 12:38–40).

This biblical event reminds me of the day when victory was suddenly announced and with it came the conclusion to the awful World War II. The joy and the clamor that broke out all over in the streets is almost indescribable. All at once it seemed as if the pent-up feelings of the previous five years were suddenly let loose—like bursting a dam. So, too, for David's people. Forgotten were the years of bitter animosity and acrimoniousness; now the tribes were of one heart and mind. Such unity may well have been the occasion for moving David to compose under the inspiration of God a song about the beauty and the refreshing wholesomeness of brotherly unity.

But there is a second occasion when this psalm might well have been composed. Seven years after his coronation David had succeeded in wresting Jerusalem from the Jebusites in order to locate his capital and seat of government more centrally in the land. He then prepared to bring the ark of the covenant into this new City of David. Then it was that they brought up the ark with an enormous outpouring of great joy.

Which of these two events it was that led David to compose this psalm we cannot say with assurance, but either will do since both are close together in time and both are marked by the same note of unbounded joy and harmony regarding the things of God.

Brotherly Love Unites and Sanctifies the Whole Body (Ps. 133:1–2)

The Hebrew text begins with the word *behold* in verse 1, calling attention to an important truth that is about to be announced. So refreshing is this first verse, said Saint Augustine, that it has been chanted by people who knew nothing about the rest of the psalm. In fact, it has been said that this verse gave birth to monasteries in Europe. It was taken as a summons for those brethren (*fratres* or friars) who wished to experience this joy to dwell together. There is no need, however, to limit these words to such wooden literalness.

Few joys can equal the joy that comes when Christians learn how to live together in a harmony and concord that can overcome every type of adversity.

Israel had had four hundred years of divisiveness and dis-
cord. After the death of Joshua, the tribes dwelt apart, each
pursuing its own aims and doing what was right in its own
eyes. There had been no common life, no common center,
no overarching authority; only strife and a constant suc-
cession of disasters attended their individual tribal efforts.
If Samuel brought a brief respite to this time of constant
bickering, it was short-lived. Their enemy, the Philistines,
could always snap their minds back to the threat of more
strife and rancor. King Saul did little to stop this onslaught
of trouble. It is small wonder then that when David brought
about a new and seldom enjoyed harmony and unity, there
was such jubilation.

So great was their joy (and ours) that it is likened to the
"precious oil poured on the head, running down on the
beard, running down on Aaron's beard, down upon the col-
lar of his robes" (v. 2). This oil consisted of olive oil blended
with the costly and aromatic spices, myrrh, cinnamon, calamus, and cassia (Exod. 30:22–23 KJV). This oil mixture was
sacred and was to be used as anointing oil. God forbade his
people to make any oil with the same formula and use it for
common purposes (Exod. 30:22–33). To merchandise it or to
duplicate it without proper authorization would result in
excommunication. Myrrh came from the sap of a balsam
bush. Cinnamon was derived from the bark of the cinnamon tree, a species of the laurel bush. Sweet calamus or cane
was a pink-colored pith from the root of a reed plant, and
cassia came from the dried flowers of the cinnamon tree.

This oil was used to consecrate the vessels of the sanctuary and the priests. But only on the high priest was this oil
copiously poured (Exod. 29:7; Lev. 8:12; 21:10).

The point of comparison between the beginning of the
practice of anointing and this psalm does not lie in the cost-
liness, the fragrance, or even in the sanctity of the oil. Instead,
the comparison lies in the fact that the oil was poured on the

high priest's head. But it did not stop there; the oil continued to run down Aaron's beard, all the way down to his garment. Thus his whole person was sanctified by it: his whole body in all its parts. Just so, all the members of Christ's body participate in the same blessing.

If the point of the comparison had been the fragrance of the oil, the meaning of oil descending on the beard and to his garment would have been lost. Likewise, had the point of comparison been that the spirit of concord descends in the state and in the family from those who govern (the head) to those who are governed, what then shall we make of the sanctity and the fragrance of the oil? Accordingly, Martin Luther remarked, "In that he said 'from the head,' he showeth the nature of true concord. For, like as the ointment ran down from the head of Aaron the High Priest upon his beard, and so descended unto the borders of his garment, even so true concord in doctrine and brotherly love floweth as a precious ointment, by the unity of the Spirit, from Christ the High Priest and Head of the Church, unto all the members of the same. For by the beard and extreme parts of the garment he signifieth, that as far as the church reacheth, so far spreadeth the unity which floweth from Christ the Head."

The repetition of the idea of descending in three successive lines is a phenomenon we have encountered frequently in the Psalms of Ascent. Surely it stresses the fact that the same oil continues running down until it has embraced the whole of the high priest. So it is with the unity of the body—God's anointing oil covers all until there is harmony.

Brotherly Love Falls Equally on the Whole Body (Ps. 133:3)

The second image is the metaphor of the fresh falling dew. Once again, the point is not to be found in the fragrance of

the gentle dew falling on the earth or in its pervasive influence. It is true, of course, that without the dew in a country
with only rainy and dry seasons, many crops would never
come to full harvest. But that is not the meaning of the comparison raised here.

Here it is the fact that the dew falls on both the high mountain of Hermon far to the north, lofty and distinguished as
it is, and on the lesser heights of Zion, the city of Jerusalem.
Hermon stands at a height of 9,100 feet in the Anti-Lebanon
range and was known to the Phoenicians as Mount Sirion.
Zion, an alternate name for Jerusalem, is only about 2,400
feet in height. But the dew fell on both of them alike. Thus
the image is exactly like the last one: the oil descends from
the head to the beard to the garment; the dew descends on
both the high mountains and the low.

What could be a more appropriate image of national concord and fellowship? As the nation was bound together by
the concord of the same dew on the high and the low, so one
life is to be found in all the members of the body of believers. As the oil sanctified and unified the whole body, so the
dew unified all by passing over all lines of demarcation, all
social gulfs and barriers of race, gender, and label.

Samuel Cox illustrated the unifying effect of the love of
the brethren for one another by noting how walking on a
crowded London street usually produced no notable effect,
even though there might be hundreds or even thousands of
people passing by. But let the Queen come riding down that
same street and suddenly every person would immediately
be bound together and declare that they too were English
men and women. For a moment all their separate aims and
tasks were forgotten as their hearts and minds were fused
(at least for that moment) into one. In that moment, they felt
what it meant to be brethren and what it meant to dwell
together in harmony. David was the first unifying ruler
Israel had had in over four hundred years. He gave the people

some idea of what it was that they could experience in their heavenly corporate identification.

This psalm, then, is a psalm in praise of the love that binds together the hearts, minds, spirits, and efforts of God's men and women. It is unity that comes from love for the brethren. This is a love that bears all things, believes all things, and endures all things. This love is a new commandment, yet it is an old commandment that we have had from the beginning. This love is a love that refuses to satisfy self-interest. It seeks satisfaction in the interests of its neighbor.

How then can we love in such a high manner? Frankly, it will always be difficult for selfish and imperfect creatures such as ourselves to love others. But if we are to have any semblance of such a pure, abiding love we must first love the unselfish Christ before we can love selfish men and women. Only as the mind, spirit, and attitude of Christ remains in us can we hope to love in such a manner. Only then will love be like the sacred oil running down Aaron's beard and like the gentle dew on Mount Hermon and Mount Zion.

Psalm 133:3 closes with one more allusion to the Aaronic benediction of Numbers 6—"the LORD bestows his blessing." The place is specifically said to be "there," that is, in Zion, where Yahweh set up the center of all his blessings for all mankind on the earth. Zion, the source of "life forevermore." This is the first place that eternal life is mentioned in the Old Testament. (The other place is in Daniel 12:2.)

Spiritual unity must characterize the church of God. Ephesians 4:3 declares that this unity must be maintained; in fact, we are to "knock ourselves out" maintaining the unity of the Spirit. Notice that the unity of the Spirit is a present possibility while we are all coming to the unity of doctrine or the faith. We do not all agree at the present time on what is to be believed (presumably because we are slow to learn and our sinfulness impedes our progress), but that should not be an excuse for our not maintaining that we are one in the Spirit. We must ponder brotherliness and cultivate its beauty and blessedness.

Closely aligned with Psalm 133 is Psalm 134, which closes these fifteen Psalms of Ascent. As F. Delitzsch observes, three things are clear with regard to this psalm: "This Psalm consists of a greeting, [verses] 1, 2, and a reply thereto [v. 3]. The greeting is addressed to those priests and Levites who have the night-watch in the Temple; and this antiphon is purposely placed at the end of the collection of the Songs of Degrees in order to take the place of a final blessing" (*Commentary on the Psalms*, 3: 321).

Brotherly Affection Gives Thanks for God's Ministers (Ps. 134:1–3)

This psalm, like Psalm 133, begins with the word *behold*, thereby directing attention to some striking announcement. It is not to the persons who come to the temple that the psalm is addressed, but to those who stay in the house of God all night and who serve (Hebrew, "who stand," the customary word for the ministry of the priests and Levites in the temple of God).

And so we come to the end of these Psalms of Ascent. How natural it is that there be a psalm that rounds out these fifteen psalms with a note of benediction. We recall how the pilgrims started out on their journey in Psalm 120 and prayed that they and their own would be protected from lying, slanderous tongues. Then we caught our first glimpse, with these pilgrims, of the holy mountain of Jerusalem in Psalm 121 as they lifted up their eyes to the Lord who was their keeper and helper. We rejoiced with them as they made their way into the gates of the city to celebrate the festival as recorded in Psalm 122. In Psalm 123 we "watched" as the eyes of the pilgrims were raised to the One who sat on the throne, just as the eye of a slave waited expectantly for some slight signal from his or her master. And now in Psalm 134 we come to the last of this series. Having heard the details of the beginning of the journey, surely it is not too much to expect that we should be given some sense of closure by experiencing the conclusion to the journey.

In Psalm 134 we meet the caravan one final time. It is very early in the morning. In the Middle East travelers often begin their journey long before sunrise—especially in the hot months, the same months when the festivals were observed. Picture a large band of travelers gathering just outside the eastern walls of Jerusalem shortly before the rosy fingers of dawn begin to light the horizon. In the quietness of the early morning just prior to when the birds will begin their anthems in praise of the Creator, the pilgrims spot God's ministers carrying out their temple tasks in devotion to the same Lord the pilgrims had come to worship. Immediately an exchange of greetings in the name of the Lord goes up to the priests and Levites and then back to the assembling pilgrims. It is a moment to remember. The songs of the priests and Levites in constant praise of God strike a responsive note in the pilgrims' souls and they spontaneously join the declarations of praise to the living God.

From the Targum we capture a small insight into what goes on inside the sanctuary of God during the long night vigils. We are told that after midnight the chief of the doorkeepers took the key of the inner temple and went with several of the priests through the little wicket of the Fire Gate. Once in the inner court, they divided into two companies, each carrying a lighted torch; one group heading west and the other east, and so they went round the court to see that all was ready for the service on the following morning. The two companies met in the chamber where the high priest's meal offering was baked and there they called out: "All is well." Meanwhile the remaining priests were rising, bathing, and dressing. Then all went into the stone chamber (one-half of which was where the Sanhedrin held its sessions). Under the supervision of the chief priest, the functions of the priests for the service of the coming day were assigned by lot (Luke 1:9).

Some suppose the opening words of Psalm 134 were addressed by the watch going off duty to the priests who would relieve them; the latter group responding with the benediction, "May the LORD, the Maker of heaven and earth, bless you from Zion." Others argue that the greeting and its response are the exchanges of the two companies making their watch rounds as they join up again. Still others view the greetings as the exchange between the congregation assembled on the hill of the Lord and the priests who had charge of the night watch. But all of these views leave out the pilgrims who had come to Jerusalem. If there is any allusion to the pilgrims in this psalm, by virtue of its context and placement in this collection of Psalms of Ascent, then the exchange must be between the pilgrims and those who ministered through the night in the house of God. Accordingly the pilgrims raised their voices as one last gesture of praise to God before they left Jerusalem and sang, "Praise the LORD, all you servants of the LORD who minister by night in the house of the LORD. Lift up your hands in the sanctuary and praise the LORD." The request is that God's ministers would always praise the Lord. Great theology must take place in the context of great doxology. People who praise little, or not at all, grow small in their thinking and living for God.

A second request and desire of the laity for the ministering body is that they should never cease to pray for the blessing of God on the people of God. Thus the pilgrims pray that the priests would continue to lift up holy hands in prayer. This is the raising of suppliant hands toward the Most Holy Place, the place of the presence of God in the temple.

The response of the priests is an adaptation of the benediction from Numbers 6:24—"The LORD bless thee, and keep thee; the LORD make his face to shine upon thee, and be gracious unto thee: the LORD lift up his countenance upon thee and give thee peace." His benediction promises that God will be good to all—collectively and individually. How wonderful it is to be *individually* assured of the divine goodwill.

The priests add, in a free use of the liturgical form from Numbers 6:24, the words *the Maker of heaven and earth* and *from Zion.* The phrase *from Zion* reminds us that God had chosen to put his presence in Jerusalem so that from that place he could bless all the nations of the earth. A local place of abode for God, however, should not be confused with the fact that this Lord is the God over all the nations. He is the Maker of the heavens and the earth. Thus he is not to be boxed in or confined to any one spot of influence or sphere of work. What a note of universalism on which to end these psalms! Nothing is beyond the reach of his hand and no one can ever successfully withstand him. He remains the sovereign Lord over all.

Conclusion

Believers must prove their love for God by the way in which they demonstrate their love for each other. How good and pleasant it is when men and women who know the Savior dwell in unity and harmony. Here is the very essence of the joy of living.

With this final reminder, we turn and with the ancients begin the journey home. It is time to encourage those who continue to minister day and night for the Lord around the world. It is time to give a word of encouragement to God's priests and servants. It is also time to remind them to ever lift their voices in praise to God and to lift their hands in prayer on behalf of God's people and his work around the world. It is time to see beyond the provincial interests of a small Jewish people at one point in history. It is time to take the salvation message to all peoples and nations in all times because God is none other than the Maker of the heavens and the earth.

Questions for Thought and Discussion

1. What is the difference between unity and uniformity in the body of Christ? Which of the two does Scripture encourage? What does this say about the amount of diversity we should tolerate?

2. Ephesians 4 makes a distinction between "the unity of the Spirit" (v. 3) and the "unity in the faith" (v. 13). Also all the verbs in verses 12–16 appear to indicate that we are all in a process of growing up in Christ and coming to some type of unity. How do you reconcile these distinctions that Paul teaches in Ephesians 4 with the urgings for unity in Psalm 133?

3. What is the connection, if any, in Psalm 133:3 between unity and eternal life?

4. What is the proper relationship between the laity and the clergy in the matters of praising God and praying for the work of God?

5. In what sense is Zion central to the program and blessing of God? Can the two phrases, "from Zion" and "Maker of heaven and earth," be tied together in any meaningful way or are they simply loose wishes that have no direct revelational association?

Psalm 133   The Unity of Saints

Isaac Watts   (S.M.)

Blest are the sons of peace
　　Whose hearts and hopes are one,
Whose kind designs to serve and please,
　　Through all their actions run.

Blest is the godly house
　　Where zeal and friendship meet,
Their songs of praise, their mingled vows
　　Make their communion sweet.

Thus when on Aaron's head
    They poured the rich perfume
The oil through all his raiment spread,
    And pleasure filled the room.

Thus on the heav'nly hills
    The saints are blest above,
Where joy like morning-dew distills,
    And all the air is love.

Psalm 134   Daily Devotion

Isaac Watts   (C.M.)

Ye that obey th' Immortal King,
    Attend His glory place,
Bow to the glories of His power,
    And bless His wondrous grace.

Lift up your hands by morning light,
    And send your souls on high;
Raise your admiring thoughts by night
    Above the starry sky.

The God of Zion cheers our hearts
    With rays of quick'ning grace;
The God that spread the heav'ns abroad,
    And rules the swelling seas.

"This Psalm, with several others near it, is called a Song of Degrees; that is, to be sung on the steps ascending to the tabernacle or temple, as the learned suppose: the king and his attendants sung the two first verses, addressing themselves to the Levites that kept the house of the Lord; and the third verse is the response of the Levites to the King. There was necessity of changing the form of this psalm to suit it to our usual Christian worship."—Isaac Watts

Bibliography

General Works

Clarke, Arthur G. *Analytical Studies in the Psalms.* Kansas City: Walterick, 1949. Suggestive brief notes on key words with teaching/preaching outlines and a strong emphasis on prophecy from a premillennial and dispensational point of view.

Cox, Samuel. *The Pilgrim Psalms: An Exposition of the Songs of Degrees.* London: R. D. Dickinson, 1885. A classic exposition of these fifteen psalms by one of the great preachers of another era.

Iremonger, F. A. *Before the Morning Watch. [Psalm 130].* London: Longmans, Green, and Co., 1917. Twelve chapters in this book select a verse for each chapter and meditate on the cry for repentance and the appeal to hope found in each.

Keet, Cuthbert C. *A Study of the Psalms of Ascent: A Critical and Exegetical Commentary upon Psalms CXX to CXXIV.* London: Mitre, 1969. This is probably the most definitive study on these psalms from a technical point of view.

Kidner, Derek. *Psalms 73–150: A Commentary on Books III–V of the Psalms.* London: InterVarsity, 1975. A succinct treatment of each of the Psalms of Ascent with several longer notes on two or three key issues.

Owen, John. *The Forgiveness of Sin: A Practical Exposition of Psalm 130.* Grand Rapids: Baker, 1977. A contemporary of Bunyan and Baxter, Owen wrote this 429-page treatise after he had been brought near to death and deep depression of soul only to find how "There is forgiveness with Thee that Thou mayest be feared."

Perowne, J. J. Stewart. *The Book of Psalms: Explanatory and Critical.* Grand Rapids: Kregel, 1989. Originally published in 1864, this exposition of the psalms still must rank among the best ever printed.

Peterson, Eugene H. *A Long Obedience in the Same Direction: Discipleship in an Instant Society.* Downers Grove, Ill.: InterVarsity, 1980. I discovered this book after I had completed writing my chapters on these fifteen psalms. Peterson has many refreshing insights that will supplement and parallel positions that I have taken.

Technical Studies

Auffret, Pierre. "Essai sur la structure litteraire du Psaume 133." *Biblische Notizen* 27 (1985): 22–34.

Beyerlin, Walter. *We Were Like Dreamers.* [Ps. 126]. Trans. J. T. Willis. Grand Rapids: T. & T. Clark, 1982.

Brekelmans, C. "Psalm 132: Unity and Structure." *Bijdragen: Tijdschrift voor Filosofie en Theologie* 44 (1983): 262–65.

Harman, Alan M. "The Setting and Intepretation of Psalm 126." *The Reformed Theological Review* 44 (1985).

Irsigler, Hubert. "'Umsonst ist des, dass ihr früh aufsteht . . .' Psalm 127 und die Kritik der Arbeit in Israels Weisheitsliteratur." *Biblische Notizen* 37 (1987): 48–72.

Kruse, Heinz. "Psalm cxxxii and the Royal Zion Festival." *Vestus Testamentum* 33 (1983): 279–97.

Marrs, Rick R. "Psalm 122,3.4: A New Reading." *Biblica* 68 (1987): 106–9.

. "A Cry from the Depths (Ps. 130)." *Zeitschrift für Altentestamentum Weisenschaft* 100 (1988): 81–90.

Prinsloo, W. S. "Psalm 126: Those Who Sow in Tears Shall Reap in Joy." *Nederduits Gereformeerde Telogiese Tydskrif* 28 (1987): 231–42.

Raffel, Dor. "Psalm 130—A *nimshal* with No *mashal.*" *Beth Mikra* 32 (1986/87): 217–20. [in Hebrew]

Starbuck, Scott R. A. "Like Dreamers Lying in Wait, We Lament: A New Reading of Psalm 126." *Koinonia* 1 (1989): 128–49.

van der Wal, A. J. O. "The Structure of Psalm cxxix." *Vetus Testamentum* 38 (1988): 364–67.

VanGemeren, Willem A. "Psalm 131:2—*kegamul.* The Problem of Meaning and Metaphor." *Hebrew Studies* (1982): 51–57.

VanGrol, H. W. M. "De exegeet als restaurateur en interpreet. Een verhandeling over de bijbelse poëtica met Ps 121 als exempel." *Bijdragen: Tijdschrift voor Filosofie en Theologie* 44 (1983): 234–61; 350–65.

Subject Index

Scripture Index

(Other than Psalms 120–134)